Note from the authors

Thank you for reading our book, we hope you enjoy it. There are a few people we would like to thank: Jay Crowter for a number of photos including the cover image, Kathryn Chedgzoy for the wonderful design, and especially Brian and Rosie Edwards for giving up their time to help us bring this book together.

We would like to dedicate this book to the Down's syndrome community, especially to new parents who find it hard to have a baby with DS. We hope this book encourages you to see Down's syndrome in a positive light.

Heidi
and James

I'm just Heidi!

Living to the full with Down's syndrome

Heidi and James Carter with Steve and Liz Crowter

Contents

Commendations

There are few people in this world as passionate, articulate, thoughtful and life-giving as Heidi Carter, who I am privileged to call my friend. In her book *I'm just Heidi!* we are given a precious glimpse into her early life. Then, in her own inimitable style, she shows how she proved those early misconceptions wrong and has gone on to live her life to the full. As we follow Heidi moving into her own flat, holding down a job, getting married, and speaking out for equality for others with Down's syndrome, her love of Jesus shines through. This is an amazingly encouraging book, and a fascinating insight into how Heidi came to be the trail-blazing woman that she is today.

Sally Phillips Actress and mum to Olly

This is a story of the heartache and joy, hopes and fears of having a child with Down's syndrome. Yet what shines through is the love of a wonderful family and the tremendous support they have received from friends, family and medical professionals. It is a beautiful picture painted by proud, resourceful and loving parents and by Heidi and James themselves. Anyone who has met the irrepressible Heidi and the lovely James will instantly recognise their authentic voices jumping out of the page with their characteristic optimism tinged with realism, understanding and faith. Those who believe that people with Down's syndrome cannot have fulfilling and meaningful lives should read this book and think again.

Dr Liam Fox MP

She charms everybody she meets, including journalists and reporters; now this book gives us a greater insight into the phenomenon that is Heidi Crowter. I loved 'hearing' the different voices in the book; those of her parents (I was moved to tears early in the first chapter)—but more importantly, getting the thoughts and writings of Heidi and James too. There's an admirable honesty in the book and Liz's observation: 'Once Heidi's mind was made up' illustrates why Heidi is a prolific human rights campaigner. Being doggedly determined can be trying but it can also lead to great achievements.

Lynn Murray Don't Screen Us Out

Prologue

In she bounced, face split with a huge, irresistible grin, laughing blue eyes full of the joy of being alive. She pushed the stray wisps of long blonde hair from her face. 'Hello, my mummy darlin. Hello, my daddy sir. I been to school. I been a good girl for Mrs Hemming and Miss Fenlon.'

Heidi was then five years old. Her podgy starfish hands poked out of bright red sleeves. They were rolled up, of course, because you can't get uniforms for reception-class children the size of two-year-olds. Still, at least the overlong skirt covered most of her legs. The veins stood out purple if they got too cold, making her look like a piece of corned beef. And, of course, we could always see the secret hidden beneath the proudly worn school emblem on her jumper—that angry white vertical line dividing her chest.

'Hello, Heidi,' we said, smiling back fondly at our beautiful little girl.

Just a simple, everyday scene, but one that had been far beyond our wildest imaginings five short years earlier.

Chapter 1

Surprise package

'Nothing can happen to us this year that is unknown to God. He knows all the way ahead that he has planned for us.'

As I sat in church listening to Pastor Paul's New Year sermon, my hand wandered down to the newly burgeoning bump beneath my dress. Inwardly I smiled contentedly. It promised to be an exciting year, with the birth of our third child to look forward to. Hopefully a girl, but I would be happy with either as long as everything was all right.

'If, as a Christian, you are anxious about the future, you are not trusting God as you should.

'Never a burden he cannot bear, never a friend like Jesus.'

I jerked back to full attention and the words Paul was quoting imprinted themselves on my brain. Later I wrote them out and added the piece of paper to all the others stuck around my kitchen. But I had no idea how much I would need to remember their truth during the year ahead.

That feeling was with me again as we drove. I had a good excuse to be going fast, and a ready retort to any expressions of complaint.

It was the third time now, but that feeling was still like no other: a stomach-churning cocktail of excitement, anticipation, anxiety, hope. I knew there would be pain—Liz squeezed my hand extremely hard at times on these occasions—but I was prepared to go through that barrier! It would all be worthwhile. The other times had been some of the most magical moments of my life; hopefully July 3rd 1995 would be another red-letter day.

So here we were in the delivery room. I hoped it wouldn't be much longer; I was beginning to feel quite exhausted. The labour had been hard going. I hadn't been able to read any of the magazine I'd surreptitiously slipped into the bag. The midwife had seemed concerned about some of the readouts from the monitor, which had been worrying for a time. The baby hadn't been as active as the nurses would have liked, but perhaps it was a bit sleepy. The most nerve-racking moment was when the heart rate dropped to zero, but apparently the probe had become dislodged!

Anyway, things seemed OK now, it was just about to … Yes! It's here! Then that agonizingly long second … 'Waaaaaaaah.' Isn't that the most wonderful sound in the world? Yes, it's a girl! Great, my first daughter! The miracle of a new life was just as powerful as ever. How could anyone see this and not believe in God? Quick check. Head, arms, legs. Two eyes, two ears, one nose. Ten fingers, ten toes. Yep, all present and correct. Perfect! Wrapped contentedly in her blanket, I held her close as she breathed in her new surroundings. So light, so tiny. Red and shrivelled, of course, like all babies are, but I didn't notice that. How could those fingernails be so small? Welcome to the world, Heidi Anne, my daughter.

I was soon on the phone: 'Hello, Mum … yes, it's a girl … Gertrude Hephzibah … yes, I am joking, it's Heidi Anne … yes, we thought so too … er, about seven pounds … hold on. (How much?) Precisely six pounds seven ounces … yes, everything's fine.'

 Male midwife indeed. He's very pleasant, but how am I supposed to relax? … Why did I want another baby? …Hope everything's all right … 'HOLD MY HAND!' and stop talking to the midwife about cars … I never want to go through this again. I must be mad, with the boys so young … Hope it's a girl … Dan and Tim are lovely but … it's all right for you, sitting there cool as you like. I wish men had babies. 'Is it all right? What is it?'

I held my longed-for daughter close to me. Yes, it was a million times worth all that pain. The family of my imagination was complete, and my world was perfect.

I lifted her to smile into her eyes; and as she gazed back the illusion was shattered irrevocably. 'Hello, Heidi, I'm your mummy,' I whispered, the sentiment freezing on my lips and a cold panic gripping my soul. *Yes, I am, but you aren't the daughter I wanted, the special friend I'd dreamed of.* I turned towards Steve, his face suffused with happiness, a picture of contentment, and smiled weakly. I couldn't bring myself to speak. Surely, I was wrong, I must be wrong. But those tell-tale signs I'd so deeply feared.

No, I must be imagining it. I'd checked automatically because this was the nightmare scenario, the dread outcome I had never been able to banish from the depths of my mind since that dream two weeks before. I must have been more worried than I had thought—that must be making me think she really did have it. I looked again, but her eyes were still the same. The dream was becoming reality.

I had to tell Steve: 'I think she's got Down's syndrome' I blurted out.

 My brain would not accept what my ears had heard. My heart was suddenly racing, my mind and face numb as I looked again at the little girl lying contentedly on Liz's chest. No, this wasn't happening to me. 'I remember being a bit worried when Tim was born, because he looked like that,' I replied eventually. 'I think she's all right.' Liz seemed somewhat reassured, but my peace had gone, my mind in turmoil. *She must be all right. Isn't she? She has to be. SHE HAS TO BE.*

The two midwives came back into the room. 'Have you noticed anything about your baby?' the senior asked gently. 'I think she has got Down's syndrome,' replied Liz. The midwife nodded sadly. 'We think she might have, too, although we could be wrong. We'd like to get the paediatrician to check her over.' Another nail crashed into our family portrait and we waited sombrely for the paediatrician to arrive.

'I hear this baby has some problems.' Her matter-of-fact tones stabbed my sensitized emotions. She didn't say, *'This baby* may *have some problems.'* My slippery fingerhold on the flotsam of hope loosened a little further. She spoke as she checked eyes and nose, hands and toes. 'Do you know what Down's syndrome means?' 'Yes,' replied Liz. Her cousin had DS. She had died at the age of three. Liz had also worked with children and adults with DS on a college placement. 'We'll do a blood test to be absolutely sure,' the doctor said, as she placed her stethoscope on Heidi's chest, 'but she has all the signs. They often have heart problems, but this one seems fine. I can't hear any murmurs.' Then she was off, leaving us to pick up the shards of our exploded world.

The following hours were a step removed from reality, as if I were an actor in someone else's tragedy. There were more phone calls, of course, the hardest

I'd ever had to make. The last thing I wanted to do was watch the child being bathed, but Liz thought we should. I suppose she was trying to take a first tentative step towards acceptance. As the nurse washed the floppy body I stood in silence and felt nothing.

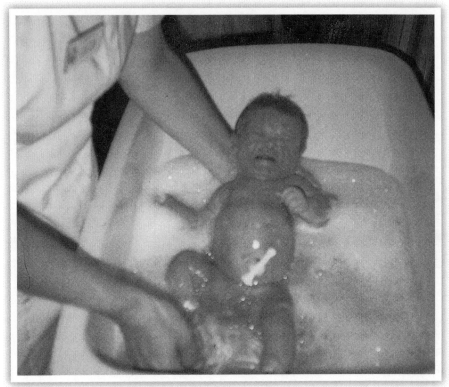

The last thing I wanted to do was watch the child being bathed

Pastor Paul

Pastor Paul came to visit us that evening. He cradled Heidi in his arms and seemed to have such love for her. I was filled with guilt; I was her mother and didn't feel I loved her at all. She wasn't the normal little girl I would have loved so much—she was something quite different. Paul reminded us of the verse from which he had preached the previous evening: 'Nothing will be able to separate us from the love of God that is in Christ Jesus our Lord' (Romans 8:39). I believed this in my head, but my heart was currently lagging well behind.

Where was God's love in this? Steve seemed not to hear a word Paul said. He just sat there, looking stunned.

Future view

'Heidi, it's morning time.' Heidi has always been very good in the mornings. Unlike some other children we could mention, she hasn't been prone to wandering around in the small hours (well, six a.m.) whistling or slamming doors. When she was younger, Heidi would sit quietly in her bed looking at books until one of us went to her. She would look up with a huge grin, delighted to see us and, excited at the prospect of another great day, cheerfully enquire:

'Hello, my friend, what day is it today?'

'Sunday.'

'Yay! Sunday today we go to church and learn about God and Jesus and see Uncle PAUL!'

Heidi has had a special friendship with Pastor Paul from that first day of her life when he held her and loved her. Of course, being a pastor, Paul has no favourites—but an observer could be forgiven for thinking that one is more equal than others.

One Sunday when Heidi was four years old we had a special sense of anticipation because three young people were to be baptized: 'There will be lots of visitors today. We must get there in good time or there won't be any seats.'

Liz was always trying to get the rest of us organized, but once again our noble intention of punctuality did not quite work out as intended. We arrived just in time and Liz went straight into the church with the other children. Heidi, true to form, chose this moment to ask for the toilet, leaving me stranded. It's always a struggle to chivvy along a child who insists on helping to flush the toilet (once is never enough) and wash and dry her hands with great thoroughness.

Somewhat less calmly than planned, we walked in through the door, her hand tightly held in mine—a lesson learnt through past experience. A surprise was in store because the baptistry arrangements meant that the whole congregation was facing towards us. I soon realized that Heidi was delighted with the new arrangement. It meant she could see all her friends, and plenty more nice people who no doubt soon would be her friends.

'Hello Uncle Paul', waving to the pastor and receiving an answering grin, 'Hello Aunty Eunice, hello Aunty Ruth.' I was frantically scanning the sea of faces. Where was Liz? Had she hidden in embarrassment and left me to it?

'Hello Tizzy, hello Baby Ham.' As soon as he was born Heidi had decided this was a far better name than Abraham. I dragged Heidi's arm back towards me as she made her way along the row to give him a warmer greeting than a simple hello.

'Hello Uncle David, hello Uncle Martin.' With the exception of myself, I realized that the entire congregation seemed to find this grand entrance highly amusing. At last, I saw Liz waving from the back row. I pulled on the chubby little hand squashed in my sweating palm, and the rest of Heidi trailed, protesting, behind. I sank gratefully into my seat.

Later, Liz apologized to Pastor Paul, hoping that his preparation for the service had not been disturbed too much. 'Oh no,' was his reply, 'I had been feeling quite tense, but I felt far more relaxed after that!' So, the episode became another example

of Heidi's unique ability to make everyone, apart from her parents, feel at ease.

Pastor Paul and Heidi

One Sunday we were delighted to be invited to the pastor's house for dinner and tea. If our pleasure may have been partially due to the prospect of a day free of food preparation, the children's was entirely because of the improved company. Heidi's attachment to Uncle Paul and Aunty Hazel was rivalled only by her love of Monty, their amazingly longsuffering collie. He must have groaned inwardly at the sight of her, but outwardly he conducted himself with admirable restraint. Immediately, Heidi was in the garden throwing a ball for him to chase. It wasn't terribly exciting for him, since the ball never travelled more than a couple of metres if it failed to hit him full on. She roared with glee every time he faithfully brought it back, adding a running commentary as excitedly as any horse-racing commentator: 'He's chasin' the ball, he's got it now, he's eatin' the ball!'

Since Monty didn't sit up to dinner, Heidi then had to entertain herself with lesser mortals. Once she had made sure she had everything she wanted to eat, she decided to impress herself on the conversation. Turning to her seventy-year-old neighbour (Heidi hasn't heard of the generation gap) she enquired: 'Peter'ogan, d'you like meat? Do you? Do you?' To Heidi, the delicious roast beef was lumped under the same generic term as Spam and beefburgers. 'I like meat too. D'you like carrots?'

'I like carrots,' a sibling managed to interject, but Heidi was not to be deflected from her task.

'D'you like soup? Do you?'

'What kind of soup?'

'Egg.'

'I've never heard of egg soup.'

'I like soup. Tim likes soup.' Turning towards the other end of the table: 'D'you like soup?' It was beginning to feel like a cross between the Spanish Inquisition and a market-research survey. 'Peter'ogan, d'you like Cheerios?'

'Yes, I do.'

'I don't like Cheerios. Tim doesn't like Cheerios. Daniel likes Cheerios . . . ,'

Eventually Heidi was satisfied that our dietary preferences had been sufficiently well aired. Her attention returned to her 'meat'.

After this episode Heidi would regularly speak to Monty on her toy phone:

'Hello Monty, how are you? Are you playing in the garden with your ball? Did you fall in the pond? OK. Goodbye.'

Monty was also faithfully remembered in her prayers, and we were reliably informed that he kept in very good health. Unfortunately, Monty's popularity promotion was at the expense of Pastor Paul's, so we were grateful not to notice any deterioration in the quality of his sermons.

Chapter 2

A hard day's night

 Back in the labour room, the staff did all they could to help us. I soon told them I couldn't face being in a ward full of other mums with their 'perfect' babies, and we were given a room of our own. I was less pleased when I saw they had put the baby's cot between our beds. I didn't even want her in the room, let alone dividing us, depriving us of the grain of comfort and strength we would derive from sharing our grief in each other's arms. We soon banished her cot to the corner and pushed the beds together.

We forced ourselves to find the Gideon Bible and read Psalm 139, though I felt really angry with God. Why me? I was only twenty-eight! One section grabbed my corkscrewing mind and held it still, though I could not embrace the depth of its truths at the time:

'For you created my inmost being;
>you knit me together in my mother's womb.
I praise you because I am fearfully and wonderfully made;
>your works are wonderful,
>I know that full well.
My frame was not hidden from you
>when I was made in the secret place.
When I was woven together in the depths of the earth,
>your eyes saw my unformed body.
All the days ordained for me
>were written in your book
>before one of them came to be.'

Despite myself, I knew at that moment that one day I would be able to accept Heidi for the person she was. Whether it would be days, months or years I had no idea. But ultimately, I too would cherish this person whom her Creator valued so highly.

We lay in the darkness as the hospital continued its ceaseless activity beyond the door of our room. Nearby, the production line of healthy babies continued unabated as we shared our sorrow and mourned our failure to achieve the expected result. *Born on the third of July— Loss of Independence Day*, I thought to myself with extremely black humour. Physically and mentally empty, our minds stubbornly refused to slow down as we sought respite. How could we encourage each other when we were both at our lowest point? I could think of only one thing which might alleviate Liz's pain by even a degree: 'Heidi doesn't have to be the last one now.'

Steve's words hung in my brain as I tried to focus on the pinprick of light they contained. Yet even as I did so I felt guilt; my disabled daughter was just a few hours old and already I wanted to replace her with the complete version. My thoughts spun and twisted with my body as I tried unsuccessfully to rest. This day had so nearly been one of the best of my life, but had turned out to be the worst. I grieved with a depth I had never known for the daughter I had lost.

Poor Heidi, she'll never be like the boys, full of life and intelligence, independent, self-assured. She won't have boyfriends or marry or have children. I'll never be able to do her hair in pretty plaits with bows because children with DS always have pudding-basin hairstyles. No chance of her going to university, or being a nurse or teacher. It's so sad. God, why have you done this?

I felt Steve against me, his body racked with sobs. I was pleased that he was releasing some of that flood of emotion: grief, anger, pain that was threatening to overwhelm us. Yet I felt so helpless. *Why couldn't I give him the daughter he wanted? Is it my fault? Have I committed some terrible sin and God is punishing me? How will I cope? I've got a three-year-old and an eighteen-month-old and now this girl who will need so much extra help and attention. All those hospital appointments she'll have, and she's bound to have other medical problems. Children with DS are more prone to so many illnesses. God, I can't do it, I just can't take it.*

Finally, exhaustion had its way and I slept a little. Frequently through that long, long night I would wake again to that dreadful feeling that something was terribly wrong ... Oh yes, I would remember, and my mind would begin again its tortured journey.

No joy in the morning

The new day dragged round eventually; the first day of the rest of my suddenly turned upside-down life. Often problems that have loomed so threateningly during a disturbed night seem far more manageable in the light of day, but not this one. As I shuffled gingerly along the corridor, I contemplated the prospect of being visited by friends. This usually gave me a sense of pleasurable anticipation, but today I didn't want to see anyone. I knew they wouldn't know what to say to me. I just hoped they wouldn't trot out the usual stereotypical platitudes about people with DS: 'They're very affectionate and always happy', or 'People say they're very placid', or 'They love music, don't they?' They would mean well, but it was the last sort of thing I wanted to hear. Although stereotypes usually have some basis in fact, they invariably present a simplistic picture, like my stupid thought in the night about pudding-basin haircuts. I knew already from my past experience that children with DS can be stubborn, wilful and exhausting, just like any other children. The sound of babies crying assaulted my senses as I limped past the nursery. How I wished I could swap Heidi for one of them.

Her brothers clearly felt she was gorgeous

I even dreaded seeing my boys. When they charged in, exuding energy and excitement, talking non-stop, it only served to emphasize what I thought I had lost. As she lay there so weak and tiny, I couldn't believe Heidi would ever be like her brothers. They were desperate to cuddle her and gave her up with great reluctance. They posed delightedly with her and us for photos. Their smiles were the only ones which were a true reflection of inner feelings. It upset me still more to see their unconditional love; they loved her because she was theirs. They clearly felt she was gorgeous. I wanted to love her as they did, but I couldn't accept her for the person she was. They didn't notice her Down's syndrome, whereas it was the only thing I could think about.

 The nurses brought us some booklets full of information about Down's syndrome. I didn't want to take this step along the road to reality but forced myself to pick one up: 'Your Baby Has Down's syndrome,' announced the cover, as if I didn't know. 'You probably feel sorrow … anger … shock …guilt.' *You're not wrong there.* 'About one in 1000 babies is born with Down's syndrome.' *So why does it have to be mine? Things like this don't happen to me; I'm one of the 999.* The God in whom I believed was a wise, loving King in total control of his universe and all his people. There were no probabilities or mistakes, no such thing as bad luck. All the events of my life were in his perfect will. It was a good theory, but at this moment I didn't like the practice of it one bit. *It's so unfair!* I read on:

'Down's syndrome is caused by an extra chromosome number 21, making 47 in all … Your baby may have delayed development … looser muscles and joints … slower weight gain … eyes that slant … a flatter than average head … a single crease across the palm …' *All that just from one stupid extra chromosome.* '… prone to chest and sinus infections … feeding problems … the body's heat-regulating mechanism does not always work well … your baby's skin may be very dry … particular attention to help control her tongue … about one in three children born with Down's syndrome has a heart defect …' *Are they more susceptible to every health problem? As if she won't have enough to cope with! Still, at least the doctor said her heart seemed all right.*

I admitted grudgingly to myself that the booklet was honest and helpful. I'd homed in on the bad news bits because of the negativity within me. But I tossed it aside and picked up a glossy little book called *Just Kids*, full of beautiful pictures of children with Down's syndrome. Although many had been through various health problems, I was surprised and impressed by some of their achievements: 'Stacey was walking unaided at thirteen months', 'Amy is two, says eight to ten words and understands nearly everything', 'Helen entered mainstream infant school at five'. Yet I was still sceptical, and when the nurse who had brought the literature came back, I asked her if these children were typical, or had they picked out the best ones to try to cheer up new parents? 'Lots of them do very well nowadays,' she replied. 'Far more is done than before to help them realize their potential.' Maybe our future hadn't been wrecked quite as comprehensively as I'd thought.

 My parents arrived that afternoon. They always dropped everything and rushed with great excitement to see a new grandchild. Heidi was number thirteen, but unlike any of the first twelve. I hadn't even been looking forward to seeing them this time. They looked shell-shocked, but tried to be positive for our sakes. 'Isn't she beautiful!' my mum said as she cuddled Heidi. I felt like yelling, 'No she isn't, can't you see she's got Down's syndrome?'

A doctor came later to take some blood for the test that would prove what we already knew. A simple procedure, you might think, but not with Heidi. She appeared to have no blood at all in one foot, so when the doctor could find nowhere else to stick her pin she abandoned it, bruised and flaming, and turned to the other. The resistance of this one was finally broken and it grudgingly yielded sufficient to satisfy its tormentor. 'But not with Heidi' was to become a familiar mantra, as every little thing became fraught with unexpected complications.

We were trying to recover from this ordeal when the consultant came in to check Heidi over himself. Then he passed the stethoscope to the student who had accompanied him. 'What do you think?' But he had to help her out. 'Would you say the second beat is a bit loud?' Then he turned to us. 'I don't think it's anything to worry about, but I'd like you to bring her back for an echocardiogram. That's an ultrasound scan on her heart.' *Maybe nothing for him to worry about,* I thought.

Heidi as a toddler

Chapter 3

Home alone

Only the day before we'd come this way so full of anticipation. Now we returned, subdued by the presence of the little burden wrapped in blankets in an attempt to keep her floppy body upright in her seat. Another psychological step: it was just us now. Yes, there would be lots of help from the community health team and family and friends. But really we were on our own. Panic rose within me. *I can't cope ... I wish Jesus would come again right now so I don't have to be a parent any more. What a terrible thought; now that's something else to feel guilty about ...*

Soon cards and letters began to arrive; first a trickle and then a flow that continued for the next couple of weeks and beyond. Many were from people we hardly knew, but over a hundred cared enough to write, from a simple thought to a three-page letter. As we struggled with our fluctuating feelings we felt supported on this tide of love and carefully chosen words. Several came from people who had been through similar experiences and brought hope that there could be a brighter future.

'A special welcome to little Heidi Anne. May you be given that special grace that will enable you to fully surrender to our loving heavenly Father, and be able to accept the little child as a special gift from his hand, albeit through tears.'

Yes, that was just what we wanted to do, but it was so hard. From deep within we were fighting against God's disruption of our plans for our life. God's grace was indeed the only antidote to this. It was a common thread in these messages. Another theme was the truth of God's loving control of all the circumstances of our lives. It was never expressed in a glib way which had no thought for the pain of our present experience. Several quoted from a poem called 'The Divine Weaver':

Not till the loom is silent
And the shuttles cease to fly,
Shall God unroll the canvas
And explain the reason why

The dark threads are as needful
In the weaver's skilful hand
As the threads of gold and silver
In the pattern he has planned.
(Anon.)

The tangled mess of dark threads on our underside view was so real and immediate it seemed impossible to believe there was a beautiful tapestry being created on God's side, though our heads knew it was indeed a wonderful truth.

'Our prayers are night and day embracing you all, and seeking to commit you all into the hands of our gracious and compassionate God and Father, who has infinite wisdom to direct, almighty power to perform and everlasting love to comfort.' Dad was not that keen on writing letters, but those he did send were always treasured for the love and wisdom they contained. It was striking how many others also told us of their commitment to pray for us every day.

Before long Janet, a friend from church, popped in.

'We thought you might like some help with cooking and cleaning and that sort of thing,' she said. 'How often would you like one of us to come?'

'That's very thoughtful,' Liz replied. 'Once a week would be a great help.'

'Oh, that's not much. We've got enough people to have someone every day if you'd like it.'

And come every day they did from a church, at that time, with fewer than thirty members, faithfully relieving Liz of many everyday burdens.

Though in one sense we were going through the deep waters alone, yet in another we were supported by a marvellous web and given great strength by its many strands. The love of Jesus was being demonstrated in all sorts of ways, from the deeply spiritual to the intensely practical.

'I'm more than happy to come up if you'd like to talk things over,' my brother was saying.

'Thanks a lot. I'll let you know.' I put the phone down.

Hmm. It's very good of him to offer to travel from London. But Pastor Paul said something similar only the other day. Strange, this sudden desire for my company. I haven't turned into Moses or Elijah overnight, so they must be worried about me. They must think I'm bottling up the emotion of this whole situation. Perhaps they are right. Am I turning all the anger and sadness on myself so that it is becoming destructive to me? I would be happy to talk to either of them at greater depth than I have done. I may do so at some stage. I just don't feel the need at the moment. Perhaps it's just me. I'm not one of these people who needs to talk and talk and talk about things. I'm often happy just to work things through in my own mind. Liz is certainly one of those people who needs to talk and talk and talk about things, so I talk it through with her. And we can share the things we wouldn't be able to say to anyone else. That certainly helps both of us.

We borrowed a daunting academic-looking book from the library. It was a bit old, and full of depressing studies and statistics about Down's syndrome and the progress, or lack of it, we could expect Heidi to make. It made for painful reading, but we wanted to know as much as possible. One particular statistic leapt from the page: 'Around 25 per cent of babies born with Down's syndrome die in infancy'—25 per cent! Maybe the book was a bit out of date, but I had no idea the figure would be that high. I was revolted by the mixed feelings this piece of information engendered within me. I would never have imagined myself capable of such thoughts before, nor would I expect anyone who has not been in a similar position to understand. But suddenly there before me was the alluring prospect of wiping this disastrous, unrehearsed scene from my play and reverting to the original script.

Yet there before me lay my helpless daughter whom I was betraying.

 Steve soon had to be back at work, finding cars for people. Being self-employed meant that any paternity leave was self-awarded and usually lasted only a day at best. Still, it did have advantages: working from home meant that he was around at least some of the time. Not that I was left alone with my thoughts; both sets of parents and my sister stayed in turns to help.

My thoughts, though, would not be thwarted. My struggle to accept Heidi was by no means won. I wished I knew how severely she would be affected. Down's syndrome always carries with it a degree of physical and learning disability, but I had seen a huge variation in the people I had known. Would she be like my cousin, who never sat up during the three years of her life, or like the girl whose picture I had seen recently in the local paper, flushed with achievement as she gleefully ripped up her L-plates after having passed her driving test? It shouldn't make any difference, I knew that, but it would be so much easier to accept her if I knew that her faculties would only be a little impaired.

I wanted to know the future, but God in his wisdom has chosen to withhold from his creation that aspect of his being. In effect, I was wanting to steal a slice of his 'Godness'. I was gazing longingly at the same forbidden fruit Adam and Eve had been unable to resist. I had to accept the present and trust God for whatever the future might hold. But I couldn't help wondering. God's perspective was unconstrained by human limitations. What could he see …?

Future view

 ### Close encounters of the absurd kind

Once Heidi had begun to talk, her streak of imaginative independence was soon shining through. One of her first words was 'Daniel', but she refused to say 'Tim', which you would have thought was easier. This made Tim rather sad. Then she decided he would be called 'Bill'.

'Heidi, it's Tim.' — 'No, e' Bill'.

After a number of such exchanges, we realized that she was not making a mistake but was adamant that she would call him what she wanted. Tim was delighted that she had made up her own name for him and happily played along with it. We soon found that she could say 'Tim' perfectly well when she occasionally slipped up and quickly corrected herself.

Heidi's great friend Aunty Eunice, a retired lady who regularly looked after her, was suddenly christened 'Cookie'. For months it was all Heidi would call her, no doubt with some good reason that she kept hidden from the rest of us.

Liz was given the title 'My mummy darlin'' and for my part I was most gratified with the respectful form of address she adopted for me. Unfortunately, calling me 'My daddy sir' seemed to have little impact on the rest of her behaviour. Eventually she graduated to the more familiar 'My friend'.

A development of this habit was role playing with the others.

'I'm Laa-Laa and you're Tinky Winky' (a reference to favourite characters from the children's TV programme Teletubbies). Or, when we hired a ChuckleVision-style four-wheeled bike on holiday, it was 'I'm Barry and you're Paul'.

Heidi in donkey outfit

At one time barely a day would go by without having the house full of Woody and Buzz Lightyear, mother and baby, lion and tiger. Heidi immersed herself fully in her role:

'Heidi, what would you like on your bread?'

'I'm not Heidi,' she would retort crossly. 'I'm Monty the dog.'

'Monty, what would you like on your bread?'

'Chocolate spread, please,' would come the happy reply.

Sometimes she would give the wrong answer to a question, just to make it more interesting.

'Have you got brothers?' provoked the required surprised reaction. 'I've got boys.'

'What are their names?' She cast her eyes around the room for inspiration, until they lit upon a lurid pink talking toy. 'Barney.'

'Barney?'

'Yes. Barney Dan and Barney Tim.' She burst into peals of laughter at her joke.

Her alternative sense of humour keeps us all amused and is another evidence of her individual character.

She would rush off behind the settee, yelling as she went: 'Don't chase me, you fruit pastille!'

We had a holiday booked. The boys bore the agonizing countdown with stoicism, but Heidi's concept of delay doesn't stretch beyond 'wait a minute'; and her minutes are about ten seconds. So, each day she would announce at breakfast time, 'We're going on holiday today. We're going to Majorca in an aeroplane.' Our efforts to persuade her that our departure was not that imminent were met with an unshakeable 'Yes we ARE going on holiday today. We're going to Majorca in an aeroplane.' Once Heidi's mind was made up, there was not much point arguing. However, she never seemed disappointed to reach the end of another day and find we were still at home. Each day for Heidi is a pleasure she enjoys to the full. The next morning she would utter her mantra with undimmed confidence.

One breakfast time we were finally able to say, 'Yes, we are!' and the children took up an impatient vigil for the taxi to the airport. The driver rolled his eyes and grinned wryly: 'You're taking that lot with you?' I discovered on the way that he spent half the year in his native Jamaica, so I guess two weeks in Majorca with kids wasn't a prospect likely to provoke too great a degree of envy.

'Let's go to the 'wimmin' pool,' Heidi would proclaim, 'and play with my friends again.' Heidi's friends were any other children who happened to be there. Her favourite activity was ducking Germans. I tried to explain to her that there was no need for this sort of thing any more, since we had actually beaten Germany the last time we had played football, but to no avail. In any case, they seemed to find her very amusing.

The kids' clubs were also popular, with the children as well as with us; and the staff always seemed delighted to see Heidi especially, despite the extra angst she caused them. One time I was regretfully wending my way to collect the girls at the end of peacetime when I found Heidi making her way determinedly in the direction of the swimming pool, having sneaked out past the doorkeeper. She made the most of her lack of stature whenever she could.

Heidi came up with various catchphrases during the holiday. The first she picked up from the club; and every time she thought we should be going out she would holler, 'Are we all READY?' With children who struggle to remember themselves, let alone all the other paraphernalia, this pronouncement was often made repeatedly and with increasing impatience before we actually left.

Whenever Heidi knocked her drink over, or drew on someone else's picture, or squirted sun cream on the floor, Heidi would exclaim, 'Whoops! I did it again!' and grin round delightedly at everyone. This attempt to disarm victims of any possible retribution for her latest misdemeanour was usually very successful. Once when she was being rebuked, she suddenly came out with 'Shut your big fat gob!' She was most gratified with the response this one got and proceeded to use it on every possible occasion. Eventually we managed to control ourselves enough to tell her with a straight face that this was not the sort of thing to say. Thereafter she just murmured it to the other children when she thought we weren't listening. Hypocritically, she was always keen to back up our disciplining of the others. If anyone dared to dispute an accusation of wrongdoing, she would call out, 'Yes you did, I saw yer!' as reliably as any hired witness.

Flying home, Heidi is supposed to be going to sleep, but is still full of irrepressible life. Finally exhausted, she shuts her eyes. I smile down at the peaceful face in my lap.

Thank you, Lord, for this little package of joy. But what about the next five years? School soon, how will she cope? Will she get left out, or left behind? What if she's ill again? Oh no, I'm at it again, trying to grab the fruit. It's easier to accept the present now, but I don't know about the next five years … or five months, or five weeks. I still need to trust God for whatever the future might hold.

Chapter 4

A sweet flower

At times, dark impulses would rise within me … *If we had a car accident and somebody had to die, I would want it to be Heidi …* This only added to my anguish. I felt almost overwhelmed with guilt because I could not yet see Heidi as being of equal value to the others.

At other moments, I would become defiant; I wasn't going to give in to this. Everyone would expect Heidi to be a failure by all the measurements of success our society used. Well, she wasn't going to be. She would walk early and talk young and pass her GCSE exams and go to university … maybe. I marched downstairs and announced, 'She's going to be the best child with Down's syndrome ever.'

Steve looked at me calmly. 'We'll help her to be the best she can be.'

He was infuriatingly right, of course. Comparing, comparing; it was so hard to get out of that mindset. I had to accept her as an individual and do my best for her, whatever her limitations might be.

I was determined to take Daniel to playgroup myself before term finished that week. Having the ordeal of facing the other mums and playgroup helpers hanging over me all summer would be worse than actually doing it, so I was going to get it over with. 'You must send her here—we've never had a child with Down's syndrome and we'd love to have her.' It was the best thing the playgroup leader could have said and I went home feeling a little encouraged.

Another big step was the first time out at church. I was dreading someone innocently saying the wrong thing, which wouldn't be difficult, and my sharp retort shooting out before I could grab it. A wise friend from church advised me not to try to answer people who made ill-informed comments about Down's syndrome: 'Just smile and say thank you.' And then there was William, born two weeks before Heidi. He had looked like a three-month-old when he was born. I didn't even want to look at him, even bigger now, healthy and perfect. I didn't know how I would bear it, but it had to be faced.

'Hymn number 320.' Oh great, I thought sarcastically, I know what that is. 'God moves in a mysterious way ...' Well, that's true enough. The tears streamed unchecked down my cheeks as the singing continued in the distance.

His purposes will ripen fast,
Unfolding every hour;
The bud may have a bitter taste,
But sweet will be the flower.
(William Cowper)

There was no doubting the bitterness of the bud; but could there really be a sweet flower? I was trying to reach into the future again, and it looked very dark.

Future view

The budding comedian

The reality was that the future had looked dark because my short-sighted eyes could not see beyond the dark present. But the bud gradually opened.

After one particularly harrowing dinner we were both feeling frazzled. Heidi decided it was an appropriate moment to stretch our fizzing nerve-ends a little further. Parents of children with DS are often rather sensitive about them exhibiting stereo-typical mannerisms or forms of behaviour and we are no exception. So, when Heidi lolled her tongue out provocatively I said sternly, 'Put that tongue away. We don't want to see it!' The offending appendage immediately popped back inside. 'OK,' said Heidi, with her usual obliging response. The problem is that the next response is usually less obliging. It gradually slid back out again. 'Less lee goo lont to shlee it,' she said. (Sorry if you can't understand her, but it's rather difficult to grin, stick your tongue out and talk at the same time—you try it; then you'll be able to work out what she's saying.) When she realized that we were dismally failing to keep our faces straight she burst into delighted laughter. We gave up and joined in. 'Show-off!' she said, which, assuming she meant herself, was quite accurate.

'Let's all have a dance!'

Due to Heidi's highly effective stress-relieving technique we felt more like dancing than we had a couple of minutes earlier.

Praying for laughs

 After dinner each evening we had Bible Time with the children (this was the aim, at least). This consisted of a short interactive Bible story, prayers and songs. Heidi was very fond of songs with actions. As soon as she was old enough to participate in Bible Time she would join in enthusiastically with these actions and the few words she remembered. For days on end she would choose songs like: 'The wise man built his house upon the rock' or 'Only a boy called David' until the rest of us were heartily sick of them. One day she decided she wanted a turn at praying. Being Heidi, she wasn't content with a one-sentence effort to break herself in gently, she went straight for the ministerial style, in length if not depth. Heidi tended to mention whatever entered her head, which caused great difficulty for the boys (and their parents) in trying not to laugh, especially as she would look round all the while, checking our reaction and searching for inspiration for the next line. When she ran out of ideas she would start all over again, until one of us intervened with an 'Amen'.

On a visit to my brother, Heidi rather apprehensively made the acquaintance of Sparky, the family budgie. For some time after this she prayed for him every night, and if anyone dared to pray for another member of the family she would add 'and Sparky!' in a piercing whisper.

When one or more of the children had fallen foul of us, which was not infrequent, Heidi rarely missed the opportunity to bring this into her prayers: 'Daniel's been naughty. Help Daniel be good. Tim's been naughty. Help Tim be good.' But, despite our joggings of her conscience, at this stage she never felt the need to include herself in this time of confession.

Sometimes she would seem to be in a reasonably sensible mood and start well, before straying into the realms of fantasy: 'Please help mummy's poorly back get better soon. Please help Peter 'ogan get poorly' (we put this down to a slip of the tongue. Peter Hogan was a man at church who was seriously ill.) 'Please help the Lord Mayor and the nightmare.' By now we were manfully stifling giggles behind our hands. The Lord Mayor had been to her school the previous week; presumably she thought the nightmare was some relation. 'Help the Lord Mayor in the hall. Help the Lord Mayor shake our hands. Help the nightmare. Amen.' We gratefully moved on to Daniel, who made the unwise move of issuing a correction by praying that Peter Hogan would get better.

'No, get poorly,' came Heidi's indignant whisper. Liz had just managed to compose herself and her prayer was in full flow when Heidi interjected, 'Pray for Jigglypuff!' (Jigglypuff is a Pokémon character). At this stage we decided that this particular Bible Time was beyond redemption.

Once the novelty of her idiosyncratic style had worn off we were less prone to fits of giggles and were able to appreciate the growing thoughtfulness behind her prayers. She would often pray for people who were ill, remembering from earlier conversations or previous days. As her understanding developed Heidi demonstrated surprising sensitivity and insight for any child, even without her limitations. Her contributions became a valued part of Bible Time.

Our flower was gradually emerging, revealing more layers of vibrant colour.

Chapter 5
The heart of the matter

 We had all the usual postnatal visits from midwives, health visitors and so on. These were more frequent than on previous occasions and always lasted much longer, as each one shared their wisdom. On day nine our first non-standard visitor sprang onto the doorstep, large as life and twice as bubbly.

'Hello, I'm Kate, darling. I'm going to be Heidi's physiotherapist.' Some months later we found out that she was known as Kate Darling, as this was her standard form of greeting. Within five minutes we knew all about her. We were delighted to find that she was a Christian and she was quite over the moon to discover that we were too. When she bounced out about an hour later we felt slightly less down than our normal still-very-low level. This was our first contact with the excellent service we would receive from the special needs community health and education team, and within a day or two we had the second. A car drew up and an elegant raven-haired woman emerged.

'Just popping in to introduce myself. I'll be seeing a lot of you because I'll be Heidi's teacher.' *What does Heidi need a teacher for? You don't usually have one of them until you're four or five.*

'I'll see her about once a week when term starts.' Since it was the summer holiday, Carole had come to see us in her own time. The years ahead would prove that this extra effort was typical of her commitment to Heidi—and also the usefulness of having a teacher when you are two months old.

July 13th. Time to go back to hospital for that echocardiogram.

We sat waiting in the bare corridor. I was so relieved to have Steve with me, yet apprehensive about what we might be about to find out. Then we were in, Heidi lying on her back, cold jelly smeared over her chest, uncomplaining as usual. We peered attentively at the swirling colours on the monitor as the doctor moved the sensor, though the picture meant nothing to us.

Finally, she spoke: 'Heidi does have a small hole in her heart. It's nothing serious. It may heal of its own accord or she might need an operation, but not until she's two or three.' *Oh no, she has got a heart problem as well as everything else ... at least it's not a bad one ... she said it's not serious ... but I had hoped it would all be OK.*

The result of the Down's syndrome blood test had come through, too. When I heard the confirmation I realized that somewhere deep down I had been clinging to the gossamer thread that the last ten days had all been a ghastly mistake.

A mother from the local DS group contacted me. It was good to talk to someone who had been through the same situation and come out positively on the other side.

'You may feel it's too early for you to cope with, but we have got a meeting this week. You're very welcome to come if you'd like to.' I oscillated back and forth over the next few days. It would be good to meet more parents and they might have some helpful suggestions; but would my emotions be up to it? I fought the fear and summoned the courage to go. There were about five mums there. After a while the conversation turned to their children.

'I'm having real problems with getting George dry at night. He's seven now, but just can't seem to get the hang of it.'

'I had the same with John. He's just about got it now. For ages I had to get up in the night to put him on the toilet.'

'How old is John?' I asked nervously.

'He's nine.'

I felt a growing panic. These were things I was going through with my three-year-old. Would I still be suffering them with Heidi when she was nine? It was clearly quite natural to the others, they were used to it; but to me it was a new and depressing line of thought.

'How does he get on at school?' I asked, trying to move the subject away from the various behavioural problems they were discussing. This was another mistake, as I soon discovered they all went to special schools. So much for increased integration into mainstream education. It didn't seem to be happening here; was it all just hype? I didn't want Heidi to be bussed off to another school, I wanted her to go with the boys; as far as possible to be like other children. But it looked as though it didn't happen; perhaps mainstream schools wouldn't have them when it came to it.

'I was stupid to go to a meeting so soon,' I thought angrily as I returned home, the future seemingly laid out hopelessly before me.

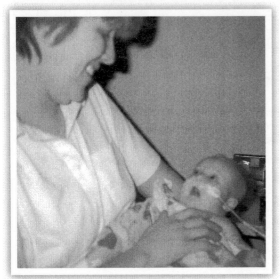

In many ways Heidi was a model baby, contented and happy enough to feed. She didn't wake much at night and slept quite a bit in the daytime, too. She was slow to gain weight, but we weren't too worried as we knew this was common in babies with Down's syndrome. July 23rd was the red-letter day when the midwife's measurement showed she had regained her birth weight.

Eight days later I took her to the consultant for a routine four-week check. He found that she had slipped well below her birth weight again. He seemed very concerned about her purple hands and feet, which we were used to, and her breathlessness, which seemed worse.

'I'd like her to go to Birmingham Children's Hospital tomorrow.' Immediately my heart and mind were racing. *To the specialist centre, and so urgently ... it must be very serious.* Too overcome with the sudden shock to take in what he said, I sat crying as his words danced round my head. Arriving home still dazed, I blurted it out to two of my faithful friends who had been looking after the boys and doing my housework while I was at the appointment. Steve was sixty miles away, so they stayed for the next hour or so, lending support when I was at a very vulnerable point.

Janet called with a ready-cooked meal for us, unaware of the day's development. By now my brain had arranged the doctor's dancing words into some semblance of order, and the questions I had been unable to form at the time were crystallizing in my mind. So Janet, being a doctor, was an ideal visitor at that moment. It was a great help to be able to talk things through with her. Only a little thing, easily dismissed as coincidence, but to me another fleeting glimpse of God's hand. One scrap of the encounter I had recalled was the doctor saying to a colleague that Heidi's liver and spleen were enlarged. I now found my worst fears confirmed—this was a sign of heart failure.

The next morning we sat in the scanning room at Birmingham Children's Hospital, watching with a familiar feeling of trepidation as the sensor was placed on Heidi's chest. What would be the interpretation of the kaleidoscope of colours this time? Finally, we heard a diagnosis with vastly different implications from the previous one. Yes, there was a hole in her heart, but it was certainly not a minor one that wouldn't affect her much.

'The heart has two collecting chambers, atria, and two pumping chambers, ventricles', the heart consultant explained patiently. 'They should be separated by a wall, the septum, and valves, but Heidi's heart has a large hole in the middle causing massive leakage. It's called an Atrioventricular Septal Defect, because the hole straddles both the atria and the ventricles, so there is leakage across all four areas. This is putting a great strain on her heart and lungs which will cause them to fail completely before very long. She will need an operation to repair the hole. However, she is not strong enough yet; we would like to wait until she is four or five months old if we can. At the moment all her energy is going into keeping her heart going, which is why she is not gaining weight. We will put her on a constant tube feed with energy supplements. She'll need to have the operation before she is six months old or I'm afraid you'll lose her.'

Our minds were reeling once again, disorientated as we tried to absorb the impact of this latest punch. But at least Heidi was in the best hands.

The best place it was; convenient it certainly was not. The twenty-mile separation from home was an additional stress on us. I was determined to keep breastfeeding Heidi for as long as possible. It had been best for the boys, and it was a kind of symbol of my resolve to do my best for Heidi and treat her in the same way as them. The closest I could get to this now was to express my milk to go in Heidi's feeding tube. This entailed staying at the hospital more or less twenty-four hours a day. We slept in a room next to the ward and Steve commuted home to work each day.

Our church helpers went into overdrive looking after the boys, cooking, ironing, cleaning more than ever. I was glad when other parents at the hospital gave me the opportunity to tell them about this, as it presented such a positive image of what a church family should be like. But I felt pulled in two directions, like a piece of elastic stretched taut. I wanted to be near Heidi; I hated abandoning her, helpless and alone in her cot. Yet I felt guilty that I wasn't with the boys; would they be unsettled staying in different houses, would they think I didn't care about them any more?

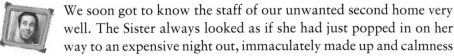

We soon got to know the staff of our unwanted second home very well. The Sister always looked as if she had just popped in on her way to an expensive night out, immaculately made up and calmness personified. The uniform gave the game away but symbolized her attitude of unceasing care towards her patients. Her staff seemed to have imbibed her philosophy of nursing, if not of face-painting. I sometimes wondered whether they cared about Heidi more than I did.

We had many visitors, who all seemed to find Heidi very loveable and interesting. One time I was sitting staring gloomily at the little figure in the cot, so thin and ill, looking at us with trusting eyes.

'She never smiles,' I said.

'You'll have to smile at her first,' our visitor replied. The point was well made. I didn't exactly feel like smiling, but I don't suppose Heidi did either.

Just William

He was twenty miles away, yet big baby William followed me. Sometimes during the long hours sitting with Heidi he would be there with us, mocking us with his sturdy limbs and healthy complexion. Jealousy and bitterness would wash over me as I fought to expel the image from my mind.

Just before Heidi had gone back into hospital, I had written to a friend far away from the situation. I had shared my feelings about William and asked her to pray for me. The possibility of a real visit from him and his parents filled me with dread, but I knew I had to resolve my anger or there would always be a barrier between us and them.

Sure enough, before long they came to see us. At first I still didn't want to look at William, but after a while God wonderfully changed my attitude. I was able to cuddle him and thank God for giving them a healthy first child. I suddenly saw how hard the situation must be for them and remembered that I had two healthy boys to be thankful for.

I phoned my faraway friend later to tell her we were now in hospital.

'How are you feeling now about William?' she asked.

I told her the story and discovered that she had spent the day before praying and fasting for me. The rapid and striking answer was another brief glimpse of God in action, like a scrap of paper blown on a gale. I snatched the scrap from the wind and held it close. Whether near or far, our Christian brothers and sisters were with us in whatever ways they could be, and our Father was at work through them and in us. Though I still could not fathom or embrace the experience of deep pain he had led us into, I knew, somewhere deep within me, that he would lead us through it and onto the far side.

Leukaemia?

August 10th. 'She still isn't gaining any weight, despite the supplements she's on,' the heart consultant was saying soberly. She had been in for ten days now. 'Her heart is failing so badly that she's using up all that extra energy just keeping herself alive. Although it would be much safer if she were bigger, we will now have to consider doing the operation soon.'

August 13th. Further news which sent our emotions into hyperdrive; thoughts of the operation were shelved. 'The blood test showed up some abnormal cells. It's probably nothing to worry about. But there is a possibility of a problem with Heidi's bone marrow not producing blood cells as it should.'

'You mean leukaemia?' Liz's voice was quiet and colourless but assaulted my eardrums as if it were a fierce scream. *Leukaemia! Nothing to worry about! Whatever else is going to happen to the poor child!*

'That is a possibility, but it is not unusual for the blood of very young babies with Down's syndrome to look like leukaemic blood. Leukaemia prevents cells from growing properly. So immature blood cells can look the same as leukaemic cells. But this is not a true leukaemia and quickly resolves itself when the blood fully develops.'

'But children with DS are much more susceptible to leukaemia, aren't they?'

'Yes, that is true, but it is more likely to be just the blood picture giving that appearance. The symptom could be related to her heart condition. But I do need your consent to do a bone marrow test, which is the only way to know for sure.'

He left us, and once again we attempted vainly to comfort each other.

'Try to be calm,' I said hopelessly. 'He said it will probably turn out to be nothing. There's no point worrying about something that is unlikely to happen.' Terribly logical, but I couldn't be rational myself, let alone expect Liz to be. And maybe he was just putting a positive gloss on it, to spare our feelings until it was confirmed. I kept that thought to myself, along with others that followed. I felt very sad for Heidi, but that demon was on my shoulder again ... *Perhaps she will die from this* ... I tried to shake it off, but couldn't, because it was not on my shoulder, it was now inside my head, inside myself ... *She's got so many problems, perhaps it would be better for her if she died* ...

Better for her? Yes, it surely would be, but the terrible part was the thought that it would be better for me.

 A day's anxious wait. Knowing the higher risk, leukaemia had been a fear in the back of my mind since Heidi was born. Was this another foreboding that was about to become reality? There was nothing I could do, but my mind would not be clear of it; round and round it went like a manic goldfish.

August 14th. Finally, the doctor came with the result.

'I'm delighted to tell you that Heidi's bone marrow result is normal,' he said, smiling.

What a relief! It had just been a misleading blood picture. I needn't have wasted all that energy worrying about it. One anxiety fewer, but there were still plenty of others. Of course, the worrying did nothing to ease Heidi's problems or mine. 'Do not be anxious about anything …' (Philippians 4:6). How I wished I could obey the biblical writer's instruction, but it seemed impossible. *Oh God, help me to leave my worries with you.*

August 16th. By now I felt the tension was coming close to breaking point. Heidi was finally beginning to gain a little weight, so her operation had been postponed to see if this continued. There was no immediate prospect of her coming home and I felt I must be with the boys more, so we moved back home. Each day I drove to the hospital, but it felt a little more like being a family again.

For two weeks Heidi continued to gain weight, painfully slowly and sometimes with depressing downward blips, but the trend was definitely in the right direction. The doctors began to discuss the possibility of her coming home, but this would mean learning to put her nasogastric feeding tube down. She frequently grabbed it and pulled it out, and it would be impractical to take her to hospital every time it needed doing. I am naturally squeamish and felt very nervous about the responsibility; would I be able to do it properly?

I shared my concern with a nurse friend from church, who immediately offered to come over and learn with me. It was a great support having her alongside to help, and the thought that someone would be reasonably close if I got stuck at home was very comforting. Despite my misgivings I soon got the hang of it, together with the technical side of the procedure: operating, priming and correcting failures of the electrical pump. My teacher pronounced me competent, and I gave thanks for another answered prayer. Now I would have to do it for real, at home alone.

August was almost gone when Heidi came home, bringing further challenges. Her overnight feed was automatic, when it didn't wake me up bleeping insistently in the small hours like a non-tube-fed baby. During the day she was tube-fed manually every two or three hours, with an energy-rich concoction I had to make up. Each feed was a laborious palaver, taking up to half an hour to complete. And the completion didn't last long, as most of it would reappear shortly afterwards. This made the whole procedure rather unsatisfying for me as well as for Heidi. There was also an impressive selection of vital medicines to remember to administer at regular intervals. For my spare moments there was a list of exercises Kate Darling the physio had left before Heidi had gone into hospital. I also wanted to give the boys the time I had been unable to share with them while Heidi had been in hospital.

'Do not be anxious about anything, but in everything, by prayer and petition, with thanksgiving, present your requests to God' (Philippians 4:6). The verse was never far away. Though I was still struggling with the first part, the 'everything' was becoming more of a reality. I was cultivating an attitude of prayer about each little problem of the day, even if only because my circumstances were forcing me to do so. Drained of my own resources, I knew the truth of God's strength being made perfect in my weakness as I prayed my way through the next feed or nappy change.

'A jewel in the crown'

Sunday, September 3rd. The first opportunity for Heidi to have her official welcome into our church family. This is one of Pastor Paul's favourite duties and usually happens the first time a baby is brought to church, more commonly at about two weeks old rather than two months. This time there was not, for us at least, the usual feeling of joyful thanksgiving as we walked to the front of the church and handed the tiny bundle over to Paul. But as he cradled Heidi in his arms, the sense of a shared sorrow and commitment was almost tangible. Liz and I, Daniel and Tim sat in front of Paul, love cascading over us from the rows behind as he spoke:

'Today is a very special day in the life of this church and Heidi is a very special person. She's special to us all because she has special needs. I'm sure she's going to be a blessing to you as a family and to us as a church. We feel a sense of privilege because God has given her to us as well, to love and to care for and to pray for. Heidi is going to need some special support and I'm sure we take it into our hearts today to care for this little girl as long as her life is spared.

'When Heidi was born I was preaching each week from the book of Malachi. I knew this verse was coming up and it kept going round in my mind as I thought of Heidi: "'They shall be Mine,' says the LORD of hosts, 'on the day that I make them My jewels'" (Malachi 3:17).

'It is our prayer that Heidi will be the Lord's, and that one day she will be a jewel in the crown of our Lord Jesus Christ.'

These were no mere easy words, but a sincere promise of commitment from the church to Heidi. We knew then, and time has since proved it, that this support would not fade away after a few weeks or months. It would be a rock in a storm-driven sea, because it was not manufactured. It was the natural overflow of a love for Jesus, the one whose actions demonstrated such deep care for the weak, the disabled, the disadvantaged people of the world.

Future view

Differently able

'I'm sure she's going to be a blessing to you as a family and to us as a church.'

We had been unable then to share Paul's confidence, but time has proved the truth of his words.

There is no doubt that Heidi is disabled. Yet there is a sense in which the ugly phrase 'differently abled' is true of her. She has talents which are especially hers within our family, whether they are connected with her Down's syndrome or not.

'Are you all right, my dear brother?' Heidi's head was cocked to one side, face full of tender concern and an arm affectionately resting on Tim's shoulder. The contortions of his face began to soften, the seething breaths quietened and the clenched fists unwound. He flung his opened hands around his sister and held her tight.

Heidi and her brother Tim

We had been unable to communicate across the wall of anger, but our tiny four-year-old had scaled it effortlessly. Despite himself, Tim was unable to resist her. Someone else could have used the same words, expressed the same love, but an intangible ingredient would have been missing from the recipe. This was not a unique occurrence; Tim was going through a difficult period of struggling with uncontrollable anger. Often, but by no means always, Heidi could communicate with him when no one else could, and the rage would evaporate as quickly as it had come.

One day we had a visitor who had no hands, but in their place metal claws. Out came Heidi to see which interesting person had just arrived. *Oh no, she's going to scream and run away, or at least make some inappropriate remark … It's at moments like this I'm glad her speech isn't always very clear …*

Heidi bounced up to him, grinning broadly. She took both claws in her hands by way of greeting, as naturally as if most of her friends had this new style of hand.

Before she started school Heidi loved to go to a drop-in centre the church runs on a Tuesday morning. Some of the regulars were lonely, some struggled with a drink problem, some felt rejected by society. To Heidi they were just friends and she loved being the centre of attention as she showed off and pestered them to read books to her. If she spotted any of them at church on Sunday she would give them a great greeting. 'Hello, George,' she enthused after one service, and then, thinking quickly, presented him with her just-produced work of art: 'I drawed this picture for you.' George was delighted and the two of them chatted away happily for the next few minutes.

One Sunday two refugees from Sierra Leone came to church for the first time. She greeted each in turn, putting one hand on his knee and pressing the other into his palm. 'Hello, what's your name?' she asked, face alight with obviously genuine delight to see them. Yes, adults had made them welcome, but they were clearly touched by this little girl. Fleeing war, leaving friends and family, just arrived in a strange country so far away, they had been made to feel at home by her. She often prayed for one of them, Augustine, although she insisted on referring to him as 'Poor Gustin'.

Prejudice—something many people struggle against in different ways and to varying degrees and the root of so much suffering throughout the

Every day crammed with fun

world—is unknown to Heidi. We may rail against it from our comfortable vantage point atop the moral high ground, only to find it lurking within ourselves in another form. Even the acceptable face of politically correct society is deeply culpable, although its proponents would be mortified at the suggestion. It is a strangely warped ethos which, with one face, champions equal opportunities for disabled people and, with the other, promotes their destruction before they are born. This must do wonders for the self-esteem of those who survive the cull.

Heidi has no concept of prejudice, although she is sometimes a victim of it. She simply accepts and appreciates people for who they are. Heidi has shown me more clearly the tendency within myself to judge people by the cover or to stick a convenient label on them. Whether disabled or disturbed, black or white, militant atheist or Muslim fundamentalist, fragrant beauty or odorous vagrant, sparkling company or duller than a beige tea cosy, I want to see people as God does—all as his creations and of great worth.

'Jake is my boyfriend,' Heidi announced proudly.

'Oo-er' teased Daniel.

'Are you going to marry him?' Tim asked.

Just children playing an age-old game, yet I feel a sudden pang of sadness. From time to time some little thing chimes a reminder of Heidi's limitations. In all probability she never will get married, or go to university, or whatever it might be.

Then a raucous laugh interrupts my reverie and I see her, head thrown back as she revels in some hilarious joke. My knitted brows ease into a smile. It is impossible to be sad for long with Heidi around. How can you feel sorry for someone who has such a great time?

'Quality of life.' A well-worn phrase these days, usually used negatively. A phrase often justifying curtailing the life of an unborn someone with a disability. Perhaps someone like Heidi. It is also sometimes used to describe children or adults: 'Poor things, they have no quality of life.' How patronizing and presumptuous!

Think of an 'average', 'normal' man. He works in a factory. Doesn't enjoy it much, but it pays the bills—just. As long as the factory stays open. Those maintenance payments really eat into his wages. Why did he have that stupid fling which wrecked his marriage? Hardly ever sees the kids now. Nights out drinking dull the pain and loneliness a bit, but he can't afford them too often.

Now think of Heidi: perfectly content with her lot; every day crammed with fun; not a care in the world. Who has the better quality of life?

Surely disability is a very poor yardstick to use. Happiness, contentment, peace; these are better measures, and Heidi exhibits them to a large degree.

In an ultimate sense they are to be found in a personal relationship with Jesus Christ, who is the only way to the fullest quality of life.

Heidi and her brother Dan

Chapter 6

Catch-22

 Despite all the difficulties, this couple of weeks at home was to prove a haven of respite; an eye in the midst of the tornado that was about to grab us once again and hurl us around with strengthened force.

Suddenly Heidi picked up a nasty cough; then her complexion turned gradually bluer, her breathing became laboured and her chest was recessing badly. All the bad old signs were back. I took her to the doctor who sent me straight to hospital. Yes, she was in heart failure again and now she had pneumonia also. Once again she was lying helplessly in a hospital cot, tubes everywhere, a plastic box over her face supplying oxygen.

I was summoned to the doctor's office to discuss some blood test results. His face was grave as I entered.

'I'm afraid I have more bad news for you. The tests suggest Heidi may have leukaemia.'

'Oh, that's nothing,' I replied. 'Her blood showed a leukaemic picture at Birmingham, but they did a marrow and it was fine.'

'I'd still like her to have the bone marrow again. It's probably best for her to have it at Birmingham.'

When I got back to the ward there was a nurse from a cancer charity waiting to talk to me about coping with leukaemia. They're still taking this pretty seriously, I thought. I wasn't worried, so I sent her away. I told her they had got it wrong; I was sure it was still just the blood picture. But as I travelled in the ambulance to Birmingham that evening I was pleased we were going there, as I was confident she would receive the best treatment for the heart failure and pneumonia.

Friday, September 15th. Big, bad days were starting to come thick and fast now. The leukaemia consultant came round with Heidi's results.

'It's bad news, I'm afraid. It's clear from the blood test alone that Heidi has leukaemia. I don't need the bone marrow result to confirm it.'

At first we struggled to accept it; after the previous experience we tried to believe this was the same again. But the truth was irresistible; this was no picture, a mere two-dimensional representation of reality. It was a genuine megakaryoblastic leukaemia, cancer of the blood, with all the dreadful repercussions those chilling words evoke.

'She hasn't got much strength to cope with chemotherapy because of her heart condition' the consultant was saying, 'That is why she was susceptible to pneumonia, which has weakened her further. She needs her heart operation to enable her to gain strength, but she can't have it because of the leukaemia. I'm afraid she is likely to fade away very quickly.'

This was some Catch–22, but it was no work of fiction.

'We can try chemotherapy if you would like us to, although it is a very invasive treatment and would be painful for Heidi.'

'Is there any chance of success?'

'A slim chance. If the initial treatment were successful there would be quite a high chance of the leukaemia coming back within the next couple of years. The incidence of recurrence is much higher in children with Down's syndrome. Talk it through over the weekend; perhaps you could let us know your decision on Monday.'

Once our numbed heads began to function again they moved swiftly into high-speed mode as we discussed and turned over incessantly in our minds this momentous decision.

If there is even a remote chance, perhaps we ought to go ahead; do we have the right to deny Heidi that possibility? But do we have the right to put her poor suffering body through any more pain? Hasn't she suffered enough? Even if she came through, and recovered from pneumonia, she would still have a huge heart operation to face. Am I thinking like this for Heidi's sake, or because it would be the easier way out for me? I want us to make the right decision, not one that I've persuaded myself is best for Heidi because of some subconscious agenda of my own. Oh God, make the right way clear to us.

'Commit your works to the LORD, and your thoughts will be established' (Proverbs 16:3). The truth of that proverb had been proved in our lives many times. We prayed that our zigzagging thoughts would be settled by Monday.

'A time to be born and a time to die' (Ecclesiastes 3:2). Are we taking God's place if we don't go ahead? Are we trying to make his decision for him? Or perhaps he has made his decision; he is trying to tell us that it is time for his own special possession, his jewel, to become part of his crown. His heart is full of perfect love for Heidi; he doesn't see her Down's syndrome, her failing heart, her near-useless body. He loves her unconditionally. Does he really want us to prolong her suffering, indeed exacerbate it, probably for no purpose? What if she came through everything and then it came back in eighteen months' time? We'd be so much more attached to her. She'd have to go through it all again, then probably die ... that would be so much worse. But should that fear come into our decision now?

The first sermon I'd heard after Heidi was born had contained a wonderful description of heaven: no pain, no sadness, only perfect joy. I'd thought of Heidi then and it came back to me now. A powerful, very real image came into my mind of Heidi safe in God's strong arms. *Nobody will be sticking needles into you there, Heidi.* I felt a peaceful certainty that if God wanted to take her, that is where she would be. Yet there was also a terrible fear of losing her. As I felt this, I realized how much I was beginning to love and accept her. Yes, she would be safe in God's arms; but I wanted her in *my* arms.

Cliffhanger

Saturday, September 16th

'You know Heidi is very poorly, don't you, Daniel?'

'Yes, mummy. Will she be poorly for much longer?'

We had tried several times gently to prepare Daniel for the possibility of Heidi dying. He was old enough to be deeply shocked if his much-loved baby sister never came home. We wanted to cushion him against this potential blow but had so far been unable to communicate the message. Now that the possibility seemed inevitable, we had to try once more.

'You know, Daniel, sometimes when people are very poorly, they die, don't they?'

'Yes, mummy, I know.'

'Sometimes God takes little children to heaven, Daniel. Sometimes even babies.'

'Yes, mummy.'

'God might want to take Heidi to be with him, Daniel. It would be very sad for us, but she would be very happy there, wouldn't she? She wouldn't be weak and poorly any more.'

'God will make her better.'

Once again, that was the end of the conversation as far as Daniel was concerned. The simple faith of a three-year-old was stronger than ours; he had prayed for this, and he was sure God would answer. But today could be Daniel and Tim's last chance to see their little sister. Although it would be another emotion-shredding experience, we had to take them to say goodbye.

'No, this way, boys! Follow the green line.'

'Don't run off! Come back! You'll get lost, or crash into a trolley!'

We were somewhat surprised to find we had all made it to the door of Heidi's ward.

'Now, boys, calm down. Remember the children in here are very poorly. Heidi might look different from last time you saw her. She'll have more tubes and things and she might look more unwell. But she's still the same Heidi, isn't she?'

The boys, of course, were desperate to skip the lecture and get straight in.

'Hello, Heidi!'

'Can I hold her?'

Excited faces, shining eyes. Throats swelled, eyes brimmed as we watched. They couldn't have cared less about all the drips and monitors. Of course, she was still the same Heidi, still their precious little sister. But for us, the black cloud came down even lower, threatening to envelop us in its oppressive power. *This decision is too big for us to deal with. What shall we do?*

Some decisions about Heidi had been simple to make, even if not easy. On that terrible first day, we had both known we would keep her; there had been no need for discussion. For us it was clear cut, although for many others in that situation it is not. But if anyone thinks this decision that was pressing down on us should have been one of those black-and-white scenarios, they could not be further off target.

You'd say you uphold the Christian belief in the utmost sanctity of life ... but now, when theory hits reality, are you chucking it in? Does belief in the sanctity of life mean preserving it at any cost? Is it truly valuing a person most highly to sustain his or her life by technology when the whole body is screaming, 'I give up!'? I don't know the answer. Perhaps it is sometimes yes and sometimes no. I do know that this situation is very, very grey. WHAT SHALL WE DO?

Before long, being little boys, they had had enough. After some gentle persuasion to give Heidi more than the briefest goodbye, they were off, rushing ahead, whooping with glee, full of life and free of care. We followed, full of care, our minds left behind with the still, quiet little girl whose life had almost ebbed right away.

We shared our situation with Pastor Paul and his wife Hazel and another wise couple. Both separately struggled through the dilemma with us. Eventually both conversations came to the same conclusion and the decision became clearer. We would proceed with chemotherapy for the moment, but would stop if we felt the prognosis had become hopeless. We felt at peace for Heidi, with ourselves and before God about the decision we had made.

Sunday, September 17th. It was a welcome relief to be invited out to dinner and tea. At teatime Liz suddenly felt she must phone the hospital to check how Heidi was.

'I'm so glad you phoned; we've been trying to contact you all day. Heidi is much worse; can you come straight over?'

We rushed to Birmingham. Now that we were ready to give them our decision on chemotherapy, was it being taken out of our hands?

The tension grew by the second as we ran along the familiar tortuous route through the rambling old hospital. What would we find? Sudden relief washed over us; there she was in her familiar place, calm and quiet, looking as if she was wondering what all the fuss was about. But her medical notes revealed the truth hidden beneath the current veneer of calm. Just two hours before she had suddenly become feverish, temperature 40, pulse 200, pneumonia worse. Her heart consultant had come in to deal with it, although it was his weekend off. Now he wanted to speak to us.

'She has come through this for now, but it was touch and go. At one point we thought she would have to go into Intensive Care to be ventilated. She improved just in time, but it is quite likely this will happen again. With all her other problems, her body is too weak to fight the pneumonia. The doctor in Intensive Care doesn't feel she should go there, and I must say I agree. I'm afraid it would really be a hopeless situation, just putting her through more suffering. We certainly can't consider chemotherapy unless her condition improves.'

It seemed even more inevitable now. When they had left us the stress and emotion took over and I wept on Liz's shoulder. It was the first time that I knew I really loved Heidi; just as I was about to lose her.

Monday, September 18th. Through the night Heidi had managed to maintain her tenuous grip on the knife-edged ridge she was crawling along. Several times she had scrabbled for handholds as her temperature, blood pressure, heart rate and breathing had fluctuated, but by morning the sheer drops on either side had become a little less threatening. Her head was still under an oxygen box, but she was more stable and peaceful.

Today's shock was good news, which made a refreshing change.

'There are fewer leukaemic cells in Heidi's blood today. It is most unusual. It may just be a blip, but we'll monitor it over the next few days before we go ahead with any treatment. I suggest we review the situation on Friday.'

We held our breath through Tuesday, Wednesday, Thursday, hardly daring to believe it as Heidi remained fairly stable and the number of leukaemic cells steadily waned.

They think it's all over

 Friday, September 22nd. Review day—and no leukaemic cells left at all! The specialist could not understand it; he had never seen it happen before. As far as we know he had no Christian faith, but he described it to us as a miracle. Although many people had been praying for this very thing, although we have an unchanging God of miracles, still it was hard to believe it ourselves.

Thank you, Lord. You really can still do the impossible. Yes, I always believed it was true, but when I see it before my own eyes, in my own daughter, it really blows my mind. Forgive me for all my anger and doubting.

It's an incredibly weird feeling, but it's hard to adjust to thinking that she might live now. I'd just become used to thinking in terms of her death being inevitable. Although, perhaps, the leukaemia will come back again next week. Or next year. But God has healed her. Does that mean she won't get it again? That would be just an interesting theological question if it wasn't my child lying there. Stop it. We mustn't get entangled in worries about leukaemia. We've got to think about the future again now. The future, with Heidi. How will we cope?

We had a couple of hours to contemplate the future. Then another high-velocity ball was fired into the crazy pinball machine inside our heads. In the afternoon Heidi suddenly became worse. Her skin temperature fell so low that she had to be warmed up in an incubator. She was examined and found to be in kidney failure. No more leukaemia, but now another life-threatening condition. Oh God, what are you doing?

Yet again her condition was stabilized, and it was time for another déjà vu conference with the doctors. This time the Intensive Care anaesthetist was there too.

'Her condition may well deteriorate again due to the kidney failure, to the extent that she would need to go on a ventilator in the Intensive Care Unit [ICU]. Now that the leukaemia situation has changed, I would be happy to take her in, as the prognosis would not be completely hopeless. But you may not wish to put her through it in view of her overall condition. The necessary care would be unpleasant for her. It would be painful for you too to see her attached to so many machines, drips, electrodes, especially if it is the end of her life. You may prefer us not to resuscitate her if she is that ill. But we are very happy to do whatever you want. Have a look around the ICU so you know what it is like and let us know later.'

Another huge decision, and not much time. We forced our emotionally exhausted minds to concentrate as we walked around the ICU. So soon after the good news on the leukaemia. Every time she seemed to improve a little, another thudding blow came in. It seemed impossible that she could recover; she just had too many problems. The ICU itself didn't feel too bad. Yes, there were more machines and monitors, but the staff seemed just as caring and attentive. Should we put her through any more? Hasn't she suffered enough? But if there's a chance, we can't deny it to her.

'Have you decided what you would like us to do about ICU?'

The doctor came before we had finally decided. After speaking with us for a while, he discerned our underlying feelings.

'We'll take her into ICU and resuscitate her if we need to.'

Saturday, September 23rd. Heidi was more settled again today, the kidney failure seemingly under control. We left her sleeping peacefully and went home to find the boys.

Sunday, September 24th. The subject of the sermon in church this morning demonstrated once again God's perfect timing:

Fear not, for I have redeemed you;
    I have summoned you by name; you are mine.
When you pass through the waters,
    I will be with you;

and when you pass through the rivers,
>they will not sweep over you.
When you walk through the fire,
>you will not be burned
>>(Isaiah 43:1–2).

After the previous Sunday's experience we had brought a mobile phone with us. Immediately after the service its foreboding ring thrust us back into the furnace. The hospital wanted us to come straight over again. Heidi's kidney failure was much worse. It seemed very likely that she would need to go into Intensive Care.

Peace is a very familiar term, but the common concept of it is a limited one. Most of the entrants in a painting competition on the subject had this two-dimensional perspective. Their submissions depicted idyllic scenes; gentle streams bubbling through tranquil meadows; motionless trees etched against a backcloth of pure azure skies. But the winning entry was shocking in its violence: towering seas crashing against the cliffs, foam whipped by the vicious wind. Many who viewed the exhibits were baffled; what had this to do with peace? But the careful observer was rewarded by the sight of a tiny bird sheltering in a niche in the cliff, perfectly still.

It is easy to have some peace when things are going well. However, as we drove to the hospital that day we experienced the incredible, deepest peace which is superimposed in sharp-edged relief upon a life in turmoil. It is the peace of God, and truly surpasses all understanding. We had just received a letter from my dad which contained this line: 'We cannot tell what God has in store for many lives from the deep waters you are now so especially passing through.' Indeed, we were in deep waters, but at that moment we knew God was in total control and was working for the good of us and others, whatever the outcome. We knew he was with us, and with Heidi, as we sang our way along the motorway:

Be still, my soul: the Lord is on your side;
bear patiently the weight of grief or pain;
leave to your God to order and provide;
through every change he faithful will remain.
Be still, my soul; your gracious, heavenly friend
through thorny ways leads to a joyful end.

I'd like to have that one at her funeral. What an awful thought, we don't even know if she's died yet. I won't mention it to Steve. Quick, I'll start singing another one.

God holds the key of all unknown
And I am glad;
If other hands should hold the key,
Or if he trusted it to me,
I might be sad.

I expect lots of people will come to her funeral. I saw the tiny coffin being carried down the aisle, imagined us watching, failing to dam the tears. We *could have that hymn about God's jewels. 'Like the stars of the morning, his bright crown adorning, they shall shine in their beauty, bright gems for his crown.' Oh no, I shouldn't be thinking like this, she might still be alive. I won't say anything to Liz.*

I was so far away I got stuck in the wrong lane past some roadworks and couldn't leave at the right junction.

Why did I have to do that today of all days.? It will probably take another half an hour now. We might miss her.

Running along the covered walkway, bursting through the door onto the ward; what would we find? Would her familiar cot be ominously empty, Heidi in Intensive Care—or worse? But no, there she was, lying peacefully; back from the brink again. The roller coaster had emerged from the latest blind bend. How many more sickening twists would we be flung violently round? But we didn't want the journey to end, because it seemed that the end would be even worse than the ride.

Wednesday, September 27th. No more alarms since Sunday and the kidney problem had improved greatly. Steve was out working and I was at home looking after a poorly Daniel and trying to catch up with the hundred and one jobs that had been left undone. Despite the ongoing support from my faithful band of helpers, there were some things that only I could do.

I phoned the hospital at about 11 a.m. for the latest update.

'Heidi is much brighter today, she's alert and looking around. Hopefully she might be able to have her heart operation soon.'

I said we would be over the next day to discuss this and put the phone down, feeling much more positive. If Heidi could get through that operation she would be so much better equipped to cope with other infections. Maybe that would really be a corner turned.

But before long the ward sister was on the telephone again. At about 2 p.m. Heidi had suddenly turned blue and stopped breathing. The crash team had managed to resuscitate her and she was about to be moved to Intensive Care for further treatment. I called a friend, who immediately dropped everything to come and look after the boys. I rushed to the hospital, alone. This time there had been no reprieve from Intensive Care. She was only alive because she was on a ventilator forcing her to breathe because her straining lungs had given up. It hadn't seemed too bad when we had been round the ICU the other day, but I couldn't bear the sight of my own daughter surrounded with so much machinery, just a cog in the middle of an artificial life form. It was too much like the final waiting room. I went out and longed for Steve's arrival.

This event caused the doctors to decide that Heidi could wait no longer for her heart operation; it was now or never. Although she was terribly weak, making the operation very risky, her condition would never improve with her heart failing so badly. It was scheduled for the following day, subject to a final blood test to check that the leukaemia had not returned.

One of the crash team doctors came round and described the moment Heidi had responded to their efforts at resuscitation that afternoon:

'There we were, frantically working away, trying to get her breathing going again as she lay there, unmoving. Suddenly she opened her eyes, looked up at us and grinned from ear to ear, as if to say, "Hello, it's very nice to see you all giving me so much attention!"'

As we waited for the long hours to tick away we wondered if we would ever see her smile again.

Heidi on her 9th birthday

Future view

Carry on Doctor

That moment turned out to be one of the first glimpses of the character Heidi would become. Maybe her early months enabled her to 'bond' with doctors in general, because she has loved them ever since. This is a good thing, because she sees plenty of them and it would make life very difficult if she didn't want to go. As well as heart check-ups and blood tests, she has had regular tests of eyes and ears and complete medicals. She has also had many unscheduled visits for sundry minor ailments exacerbated by her heart and chest weakness, not to mention her visits to a paediatrician regarding an ongoing constipation problem. She is always most indignant if another member of the family goes to the doctor without her, and even the dreaded injections have failed to dim her enthusiasm for medical people.

'I'm going to the doctor's to see the nurse,' she announced excitedly to everyone she met that morning. You wouldn't be so chirpy if you knew what you were in for, I thought grimly. My stomach was beginning to knot at the prospect. I was taking two of them to do a job lot, so it would be double trouble for me. The waiting room was crowded and we had to squeeze into a narrow gap on the seat. The man next to us didn't see any need to move up, but Heidi soon found a solution.

'Here you are man, read this.' She picked up the magazine that sat between us and him, plonked it down on his lap and planted herself in the space thus liberated. Thankfully he was amused and after a few minutes we noticed he had obeyed her instruction and was absorbed in an article.

When the dreaded moment came Heidi greeted the nurse with great enthusiasm, took her hand and went into the surgery like a lamb to the slaughter. She watched in open-mouthed amazement and growing disapproval while her sibling kicked and yelled as the sleeve was yanked up, then screamed without drawing breath for two minutes after the event. When it was finally her turn, Heidi held out her arm keenly and grinned at the nurse.

'Oh, don't,' the nurse groaned. 'I always feel guilty doing this and you're making it even worse.'

I shut my eyes and prepared for the howl as the needle pierced her skin, but she just flinched slightly and didn't make a sound. Maybe after everything she has been through it didn't seem a big deal.

'Goodbye, nurse, see you soon,' chirped Heidi, grin still at the ready. 'Thank you for giving me my 'jection.'

Soon after Heidi started school she had to make one of her visits to the paediatrician about her constipation. This time there was a young man with the doctor.

'Would you mind if I used Heidi to show my student some features of Down's syndrome?' she asked. I replied that it was fine.

'The first thing to notice is this,' the paediatrician said, pointing to the badge on Heidi's school jumper. 'Many children with Down's syndrome now go to a mainstream school and integrate very well.'

Heidi delightedly showed off hands, face, chest, limbs and so on, pleased as ever to be the centre of attention.

'Well done, Heidi, you're a star,' said the doctor when she had finished.

'I'm not a star,' retorted Heidi indignantly. 'I'm a superstar!'

On the next visit a junior doctor was present.

'Hello, lady,' said Heidi cheerfully to the paediatrician, and, turning to her colleague, 'Hello, doctor.'

'The lady's a doctor too, Heidi,' I quickly chipped in.

'No she's not, she's a lady,' returned Heidi emphatically. I knew that trying to persuade her otherwise would be futile.

'It's because you haven't got a stethoscope,' I explained apologetically.

When she had been examined Heidi turned to the junior doctor while the paediatrician discussed Heidi's condition with me.

'Can you read these books to me?' she asked, with irresistible pleading eyes.

Finally we were ready to go.

'Say goodbye, Heidi.'

'Goodbye, doctor. Thank you for reading books to me. Goodbye, lady.' Then, not wishing to be impolite, 'Thank you for … er … thank you for … er …' Suddenly inspiration struck, and with a big grin: 'Thank you for lookin' at my bottom!'

Our GPs are all very interested in and fond of Heidi. After one cheerful, chatty encounter, the doctor commented, 'You know, with all her limitations, I'm sure Heidi is more like God meant us to be than most of us are.'

Back to the future

Thursday, September 28th. The blood test was clear; the operation was on. Steve's parents and mine came up and sat with me through the interminable hours Heidi was in theatre. Steve had to work and would arrive later. He'd said, with typical male logic, that he couldn't do anything while they were operating anyway, but I still wished he was there. Eventually he arrived and after further waiting the surgeon came out.

'The operation was successful, and Heidi has been stable since she has come back to ICU. It was more complicated than we were expecting. We haven't been able to seal completely the leak in one valve, but there is only minor leakage now. She will need another operation on this when she is two or three. She's not out of danger yet, but she's a real fighter. I'm confident she'll pull through.'

As we rejoiced and thanked God we saw what so easily could have been us: a young couple, distraught, vacant, disbelieving. Their news had been so different. No doubt they too had been to some extent prepared for it, yet the finality of death was still deeply shocking. Our hearts went out to them. We could so easily empathize with their feelings of empty despair which we had been so narrowly spared.

Over the following days Heidi slowly but surely gained strength. As expected, she was in ICU for longer than the usual time. This was due to her extreme weakness when she had the operation. However, on October 5th she returned to the children's ward and after a further ten days she was well enough to come home.

While she had been in hospital there had always been the thought that she might relapse again. After so many such experiences it was hard to come away from that mindset. Psychologically, the move home again seemed to be the last hurdle. We started to allow ourselves to believe that she really would survive.

Yes, I've got to love and accept her fully now. I've not had to think in those terms recently, but she's with us for keeps—or at least for the moment. That placard inscribed 'LEUKAEMIA' in big black letters was up in the back of my mind again, as it has been periodically to this day. *After all we've been through, it shouldn't be a difficulty to accept her. God has given me my daughter back from the dead! Oh Lord, I am so thankful, I really am. If you had not been guiding our decisions, we wouldn't have her now. If we'd given her up when it seemed so hopeless; if we'd said no to resuscitation in ICU. It doesn't bear thinking about. I do love her, but she's still got Down's syndrome, she still needs tube feeding, she's still going to be so demanding. Oh Lord, help me to cope. Help me to accept her. Help me to value her as much as I value the boys.*

Stares in their eyes

Just one week of having Heidi at home and it was half-term. Like a couple of idiots we decided it was a good idea to go away, so off we set for Wales in the small hours. Heidi's night-time continuous tube-feeding contraption was stuck in place above her seat. It felt great to be going on holiday, until we stopped for breakfast at a Bad Cook, or whatever those roadside restaurants are called. Steve got Heidi out of the car, but forgot about her inseparable companion, the milk machine. I crouched in the freezing cold car park for the next ten minutes, threading the tube back down Heidi's throat, reattaching the tube to her face (two layers of different sticky tapes to avoid damaging her skin) and re-priming the pump so it didn't turn itself off.

We were feeling rather less relaxed by the time we finally made it inside. But inside was ten times worse. As we stepped through the door a sudden deathly hush descended. Servers stopped serving in mid-splat and waitresses stood stock still, although that was hardly noticeable. Everyone in the cafe swivelled towards Heidi, their eyes stuck out on stalks as they gawped in tasteless fascination. No, of course I was not in the least oversensitive, neither am I exaggerating at all. As we clattered our way towards the partial relief of a table, anger and hurt welled up with the tears. I felt like screaming at them, 'Yes, she's got Down's syndrome! And sticky tape on her face! Have a good stare, why don't you!'

I sank into a seat and buried my head. *Whatever made me think it was a good idea to go away? This is going to be a nightmare, people staring at her all week. It's not fair! Why does she have to have Down's syndrome? Why can't she be a lovely, normal baby, with people cooing over her? Why does she have to have this horrible ugly pump and tube? I want to go home and shut myself away ...*

Everyone in the cafe swivelled towards Heidi

'BLEEP! BLEEP! BLEEP!' *That stupid pump! What's gone wrong now?* The eyes all swung smartly round to attention. 'I hope they rick their necks,' I thought, as I took the stage once more to remove the airlock which had triggered Act Two. *Let them stare. I'll show them I can sort this out calmly and efficiently.*

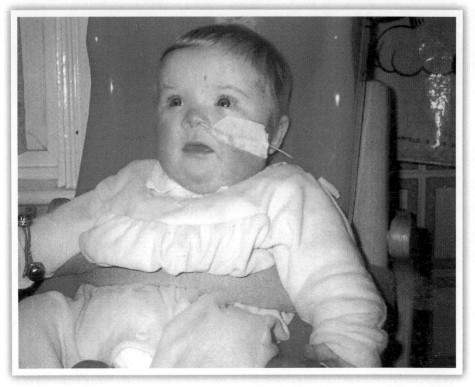

Things could only get better, and thankfully they did. There were lots of things for the children to do at the caravan park where we were staying, and they loved playing together. I still noticed people staring at Heidi, or else quickly looking the other way. They couldn't win, really. Steve said it was just human nature, they weren't meaning to be rude. I tried to ignore it and managed to cope, most of the time.

We came across another little girl with DS in the soft play area. She was about a year old, crawling around and having great fun. Her older brother and sister were playing with her and clearly adored her. We chatted to her parents who were very happy and positive about her. It made me feel a little better myself, until Steve pointed out an older girl who also had DS. She had what I thought of as a stereotypical DS haircut and glasses. What a hypocrite I was, putting her in a box straightaway. She was about ten, but playing at a far younger level. The negativity came flooding back; I wanted Heidi to be capable and attractive, not left behind and labelled. I was going to do everything within my power to help her achieve what I wanted, but would she ever reach my aspirations? I wanted to stop watching the girl who was unwittingly saddening me, but I couldn't. My eyes were magnetized, although, of course, I didn't stare.

It's still a struggle sometimes. One day I came back fed up and exhausted after a marathon session at Safeway's.

'Stare, stare, stare!' I let off at Steve. 'Why do people have to do it? Haven't they seen anyone with Down's syndrome before?'

'They were probably staring at you,' Steve replied nonchalantly, without interrupting his gaze at the newspaper. The remaining steam dissipated rapidly as I preened myself.

'Thank you, darling,' I simpered.

'No, I meant they were probably thinking, "Why ever is that barmy woman dragging four kids round a supermarket?"'

He's so unobservant he never notices anyone staring in any case. Typical insensitive man.

Chapter 7

Small steps to normality

 We woke up the next morning feeling that the time away had done us good. Hopefully we would have a stable period now to get used to having Heidi around and rebuild our family equilibrium.

Later that day Heidi developed a bad cough. Her breathing became laboured, her complexion deteriorated and the following day she was once more in hospital with pneumonia. For a while it was touch and go again; had she been given back to us just to be taken away? But this time the antibiotics were able to take effect. Now that her heart was working properly her still-tiny body had enough strength to fight the infection. For a long time her lungs were still a weakness, so that any infection rapidly became pneumonia. Nevertheless, she made it through the winter with only two more short stays in hospital.

There was still a great deal more to do for Heidi than for a healthy baby. She was still being tube fed by the wretched unreliable pump overnight and the even more detested manual method by day. There were lots of appointments with teacher, physiotherapist, dietician, speech therapist, health visitor, hearing specialist and sundry doctors. These were often helpful, but all took time and usually left me with a 'homework sheet' of exercises or targets to pursue with Heidi.

Since Heidi had come home after her operation Kate, the fizzy physio, had been bounding in about once a fortnight and Carole the teacher had been calling each week. The first few months of Heidi's life had done nothing for the poor muscle tone that is characteristic of babies with Down's syndrome, or for her general development. She had missed some of the important early progress and we now needed to try to make up for lost time.

Kate and Carole gave us complementary programmes of exercises for Heidi to stimulate her mental and physical development. The approach was to prepare her to reach the standard milestones that most children achieve naturally. Hopefully with this assistance she would not be too far behind. Carole spent many hours on her knees patiently encouraging Heidi to look at a mirror or hold a rattle. Early targets were to focus on a brightly coloured toy, then follow it from side to side, then reach out for it. Carole shook and banged toys above Heidi to encourage her to raise her head when lying on her tummy. She placed objects just out of reach so Heidi had to move to get them. At about six months Kate provided a soft 'tumble form' chair so Heidi could sit fairly upright. This enabled Heidi to learn to bang toys on a table, a skill I sometimes felt could have usefully been left untaught! Heidi loved these weekly sessions and her friend Carole seemed equally enthusiastic.

Big brother Tim was often around and was naturally intrigued by the proceedings. He was very keen to 'help' Heidi with her tasks. My role was to distract him by reading endless books, while still taking in and remembering the exercises to repeat and repeat and repeat during the coming week. Each term Carole prepared a detailed list of activities, so I always had this to fall back on if my memory failed.

It was a constant struggle to squeeze the exercises into hours which seemed far shorter than they used to be. When I failed to do so I felt I was letting Heidi down and that if she failed to fulfil her potential it would be my fault. When I succeeded, I often felt depressed; her poor floppy limbs seemed so slow to fill out and strengthen despite so much attention. Her targets sometimes seemed like specks on the horizon which never came closer.

Yet as she grew more able to express herself, her ready smile and laugh would soon cheer me up. When she finally did manage some small thing, to grab a toy or roll over or sit up, the long weeks of frustration fruited in an intense joy at her great achievement.

A speech therapist also came sometimes. Her first task was to get Heidi to drink so she could be weaned from her tube. Like talking, it is all to do with making the right shape with your mouth. You probably don't know how many different shapes, sizes and designs of bottle teats and feeder cups are available, because most babies aren't too bothered. We amassed what was probably the most valuable collection in the world, but to no avail. Heidi was quite happy eating cereals, bananas or cauliflower, but give her a bottle to suck and she didn't want to know, whether the teat was shaped like a nipple or an elephant's trunk. As a result Heidi was nearly a year old before the pump and tube were finally jettisoned and the speech therapist was able to concentrate on speech.

'Encourage listening and copying sounds which you and Heidi enjoy,' as she put it. I sometimes felt I was approaching the limits of my mental tether, but I am thankful to say that Heidi's pleasure in saying 'oo ah ba ba da da' appeared greater than mine.

Two mad parents and another baby!

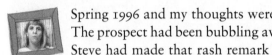Spring 1996 and my thoughts were turning towards another baby. The prospect had been bubbling away in the back of my mind since Steve had made that rash remark on the day Heidi was born. He was not going to be allowed to forget it. At first it had been another guilt-tripping way to escape from reality. I had been thinking about another child as a replacement for the damaged goods I had unwrapped; the next one would be the perfect daughter Heidi should have been.

Am I still thinking like that underneath? I worried sometimes, especially when I was exhausted from a frustrating session with an unresponsive Heidi.

'Is it wrong to want another baby?' I asked Steve.

'Not necessarily,' he replied cautiously, knowing what was coming up, but honesty preventing him from being too negative.

'When I think about it, I always visualize a daughter who will be as I wanted Heidi to be; and then I feel bad. It seems as if I can't really have accepted her if I want another one.'

'But you don't want to replace her, do you? It's not as if you're going to trade her in for the new improved model.'

'No, I can't bear to think of losing her now. I love her so much.'

'You have accepted her for who she is, then, haven't you?' Steve replied gently. 'That doesn't make it wrong to want another child to love for who she is, or he is.'

'You did say, "Heidi doesn't have to be the last one now".'

'You've made sure the words are burned into my brain, dear.' Not quite so gentle now. He quickly went on: 'But there's no hurry, you've got so much to cope with. Daniel's not even four and Heidi will be very hard work for a long time yet. You wouldn't want another baby when Heidi is still like a baby herself.'

'They do take nine months, you know. And I might take a few months to get pregnant, and the others are only about eighteen months apart. I wouldn't want her ... I mean, I wouldn't want the baby to be all on its own, much younger than the others.'

'I wasn't suggesting waiting five years. Heidi will develop more slowly anyway. The next one will catch her up, so it would be a good thing to wait a bit longer.'

Ouch. That was something I was dreading already. I had to admit grudgingly, in my more rational moments, that Steve's arguments made sense. But I hate waiting for things. Now I'd started thinking about it, I wanted to get on with it.

Soon I had some good news to tell Steve, which elicited a predictable 'I told you so'. But my excitement was mingled with a deep fear.

'I hope the baby's all right,' I would say to Steve.

'You know Heidi hasn't got the hereditary form of Down's syndrome. There is only a slightly increased chance for subsequent pregnancies. It is incredibly improbable to have two babies with DS.'

'I know the statistics,' I wailed, 'but I just can't help worrying about it.'

Steve put a comforting arm around me. 'But we have proved God is faithful over the last year or so. We must try to trust him with this baby. He won't let us suffer more than we are able to bear, he has promised that in the Bible.'

The only 'cure' for Down's syndrome and other 'foetal abnormalities' is termination of pregnancy, the destruction of a life created by God in his image, even if not up to society's standards. So, there had never seemed much point in having the AFP blood test for these things. I had asked my GP to put in my notes that I did not want it. There had been no pressure at the twelve-week scan when it would normally have taken place, but I feared the gynaecologist would not leave it at that. 'Mrs Crowter,' I imagined him saying, 'one child with Down's syndrome is enough for anyone. Don't you think you have been a little foolish in refusing the AFP? It's too late for the AFP now, but we could go straight on to an amniocentesis. I think you should seriously consider it.'

I had been praying that I wouldn't be pressurised about it, but it was still with some trepidation that I went into the room. As usual, although it was a consultant appointment, I would only get to see his sidekick. I hadn't seen the doctor before, but his smile was friendly as I surveyed him warily.

'Mrs Crowter,' he said. 'That's an unusual name. Is your husband's name Steve?'

I looked up, startled. What did they teach at medical schools these days, mind-reading?

'Yes, it is, actually.'

'Did he go to school in Kingston?'

'Yes, he did.' It was becoming, I imagined, a bit like a visit to a fortune teller, but with more accuracy and without the palm-tickling nonsense.

'I was at school with him. What's he up to these days?'

We started chatting and immediately the tension slid away.

'I see from your notes that you didn't have the AFP test. You know all about it, do you?'

I explained my reasons for not having it. He would have known what Steve's views on abortion were, so he was not at all surprised. There was no attempt to persuade me otherwise, nor the least implication that I was foolish. I went home with a great sense of relief. God has many ways of answering prayer and I really appreciated that one.

It was an ongoing struggle to trust God and not worry, although the pregnancy progressed smoothly. I was delighted to feel the baby moving and kicking, but I would rapidly become concerned if it had a rest. I became like a crazed sergeant major, expecting a twenty-four-hours-a-day exercise regime. With the benefit of hindsight I knew Heidi had been less active than the others, so I was very sensitized to the movement of this one.

Finally, the time came and we were making that familiar journey once more. Now it was so close my fears were pressing in on me again. I couldn't wait until it was over. Hopefully it wouldn't be too long, being a fourth child.

But my hope was far from fulfilled. The contractions stopped as soon as we arrived and we ended up wandering around the hospital for half the morning, hoping the movement would get things going again. Eventually we made it to the delivery room, but after four hours in there I was beginning to panic.

'Is everything all right?'

'Yes, it's fine,' the midwife replied soothingly. My worries, though, would not be quelled. Was she just trying to keep me calm? She seemed to be paying a lot of attention to the monitor showing the baby's heart rate. *This isn't right, there must be something wrong with the baby ... hang on, I think it's coming at last ... yes ...*

'Has it got Down's syndrome?' I blurted.

'It's a girl!'

'HAS IT GOT DOWN'S SYNDROME?'

'She doesn't have any of the characteristics of Down's syndrome. You've got nothing to worry about,' said the midwife calmly. At last, after all these months of having that thought gnawing away, I was free. Deep relief washed over me with the exhaustion.

'Did you say it's a girl?' Now I could appreciate it. I held Suzanna close and looked into her eyes. The last lagging doubts drained away as I saw for myself that it was true. I took her little legs in my hand. They were firm and strong. I unrolled the fingers wrapped tightly around mine. No unbroken crease across the tiny palm. *Thank you, Lord.* 'It's just what I wanted' has never rung more true. Now my family really was complete. Not the one I'd imagined, but the one God had chosen for me and with which I was perfectly happy.

'Now I know why she was such a long time coming.' The midwife was holding up an umbilical cord with a knot in the middle. 'This is what we call a true knot. It's not just a loop. See how tight it is. It makes it harder for the oxygen to get through to the baby. I was getting concerned that she was becoming unreactive towards the end, as if she was going to sleep. I was only seconds away from taking you for an emergency Caesarian when she finally decided to arrive.' So, she *had* been putting on the 'no-worries' line. Steve and I smiled weakly at each other, even more thankful now for the safe birth of our daughter.

'It's very rare.' The midwife was still holding the cord. 'Do you mind if I take it to show my student?'

Despite the complications Suzanna and I both made a rapid recovery. Later on a nurse came to ask if I would like to go home or stay in hospital for the night.

'I'll get more peace here if I can have a room on my own,' I replied. 'If I'm on a ward I won't sleep at all, so I'd rather go home.'

There was a room available, but I still had a bad night. I couldn't blame Suzanna; she slept very well. The problem was that I kept waking up, and every time was unable to believe what my befuddled brain was telling me. I had to get out of bed, go over to the cot and check that she really was a healthy little girl.

Steve came the next day with the others. The boys, of course, rushed in full of excitement. But as I saw Heidi being carried in Steve's arms the reality of the situation suddenly struck me like a fist in my sensitive solar plexus. *What have I let myself in for? A brand new baby, and another one who still can't walk! Why didn't I listen to Steve?*

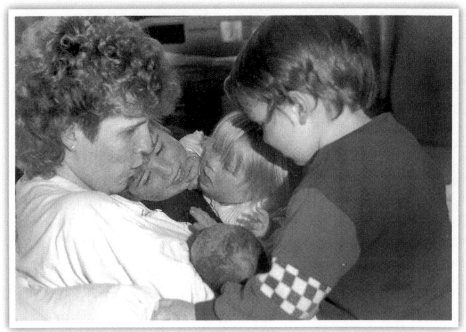

'Those are Suzanna's eyes, Heidi, no, don't poke them'...

I didn't have long to panic because they were all over Suzanna, grabbing, stroking ... 'Those are Suzanna's eyes, Heidi, no, don't poke them'... patting, hugging ... 'Be gentle, Heidi, she's not a teddy bear' ... kissing, touching ... 'Those are her ears, Heidi, DON'T PULL THEM'.

For the first time in her life Heidi seemed big as she explored her wonderful new toy, grasping the tiny fingers in her huge chubby fist, threatening to squeeze the life out of Suzanna's delicate form as she enveloped her delightedly in a sisterly hug.

Steve was telling me what had happened after he had left me the day before and gone to collect the boys from their temporary guardians: 'When I told the boys the news, Tim rushed off yelling excitedly, "We've got a baby sister and her name's Hosanna!"' I laughed happily at the delicious mistake. We both felt like singing loud hosannas of praise to our God for his perfect gift. *With God's help, we'll cope with our four little bundles of trouble and joy*, I thought contentedly.

We only became aware of the full significance of the umbilical cord knot a few days later when I was back at home. I was recounting my birth experience to the visiting midwife. Her eyes widened in surprise.

'Was it a true knot?'

'Yes.'

'Wow, someone was looking after you.'

She told us that the knot becomes tighter and tighter as the baby moves around. Often this restricts the blood flow so much that the baby dies or is brain-damaged. I looked down at my precious, perfect daughter. Yes, Someone certainly had been looking after us and her.

Heidi and Suzie

End of an era

 Yet again Heidi and I were making the familiar trip to Birmingham. The car was on autopilot and my thoughts were free to roam. It was two years since Heidi's operation and time for another six-monthly check-up. Yes, this was just a routine visit and Heidi seemed to be in good health. There was no reason to worry, and yet my adrenaline level was up. It was partly an automatic response to driving this route; yet it was more than that. What if they found a problem? I couldn't bear to think about it, but I couldn't help thinking about it.

'Mrs Crowter, please come through.' At last, the wait was over. I took the seat the consultant indicated and awaited the verdict.

'I'm delighted to say Heidi is in very good shape.' I exhaled the tension as he continued. 'There is still a little leakage from one of the valves, but it's nothing to worry about. She shouldn't be needing another operation for the foreseeable future. In fact, I don't think we need to see her again for two years.'

Suddenly I felt exultant. Every six months had implied some degree of concern about Heidi's heart; there was always an appointment looming. The fear that she might need that second operation had always been there. Two years was almost a discharge.

'Thank you for all you have done for her, doctor.'

In a sense it was the end of an era. My mind ran back over the past two and a half years of involvement with the hospital. Heidi had been given nothing but love, respect and the best treatments available. Thanks to that I still had my daughter. *Thank you, Lord.*

Chapter 8

The long journey to school

 'I love the sound of Heidi's laugh. Life would be so dull without her, wouldn't it? We'd just wake up in the morning and think, "Oh well, another dull old Monday".'

Tim's unprompted comment neatly summarised the extra dimension Heidi brings to our everyday family life. Life is rarely easy, but it is certainly never dull. I thought back to the seemingly interminable process leading up to Heidi starting school: by turns frustrating, depressing, wearing, yet lightened by Heidi's unfailing cheerfulness and enthusiasm, and the caring commitment of so many of her professional helpers.

The scenario had seemed so clear cut with the boys. When the time came they went to playgroup, then school. It just happened; there were no issues or complications. With Heidi, the saga began much earlier. She started nursery when she was about a year old, so before then we had to decide where she should go. Heidi's teacher Carole took me to see the different options, and the choice we made proved an excellent one. It was a mainstream nursery, but the two sessions each week that Heidi attended were for children with special needs. Her band of professional helpers were able to go in and see her there, often having group sessions with others of their 'clients' who also attended the nursery. I appreciated these periods of respite even more after Suzie arrived on the scene. The pressure to practise Heidi's various exercises was also eased by the knowledge that the dedicated nursery staff were filling her time there so positively, using the programmes provided by her professionals and other stimulating activities.

Carole still came to visit Heidi at home too. By now they had moved on to posting, first balls and then shapes. Over the next year they did three-, four-, then five-piece jigsaws. They rolled a ball to each other, although sometimes the roll would turn into a throw and Carole would become a target. They practised language using picture cards: recognizing, then pointing, then copying the sounds. Carole's target sheets became Individual Educational Plans, running to five or six A4 sheets of specific exercises designed to work towards Heidi's targets. These would cover all developmental areas:

- Language and Literacy (e.g. pointing to body parts). Heidi's speech therapist also called every six weeks or so and worked on this area in conjunction with Carole.

- Mathematics (e.g. building a tower of three bricks).

- Physical (e.g. walking holding someone's hand).

- Personal and Social Development (e.g. pouring water).

Carole meticulously recorded Heidi's progress, or lack of it, in each activity week by week. By the age of two Heidi was beginning to say a few words and walk with a baby walker, legs wide apart due to her continuing muscle weakness. It was a long process to train those legs to straighten. She chose Christmas Day 1997, before an admiring audience of cousins, uncles, aunts and grandparents, to take her first solo steps. Revelling in the reaction this produced, she carried on right across the room. It had taken two and a half years, but after that there was no stopping her.

In January, Heidi started at the playgroup the boys had been to, as well as her two mornings at the special needs nursery. The leader was delighted to take her, true to her word to me in those first weeks of Heidi's life. She was the first child with DS to go there, but they were more than happy to make the extra effort necessary. It was another opportunity for Heidi's stimulation, progress and fun.

Almost immediately it was time to start making decisions again, this time regarding the nursery for her pre-school year starting in September. It seemed impossible that this could be coming around so soon,. However, being born in July meant that she would be one of the youngest in her year. She could go to the nursery attached to a school for children with moderate learning difficulties. The natural progression from there would be to move on to that school, although that did not have to

Heidi's teacher, Carole

happen. The main alternative was a new service called an Enhanced Resource Nursery. This was a mainstream nursery, but with provision for six children with special needs among the twenty or so others. The success of this system was subsequently illustrated by the comment of another prospective parent being shown around: 'It looks very good, but where are the children with special needs?'

In effect the decision was not just for the coming year, but possibly for the whole of Heidi's school life. Did we want her to go to a special needs school? Classes would be small. The whole system would be designed with special needs pupils in mind. She would be working with children of a similar ability level. The school had a good reputation.

Once again Carole took me to see the two nurseries. I was impressed with both, but which would be the best for Heidi? We wanted her to be fully integrated into society one day; surely it was best to start the process as soon as possible. Another line of thought was that Heidi was always observing and imitating others. This was often a good thing, although it did mean she picked up our boys' bad habits. In a mainstream environment we hoped that she would be helped by trying to copy others whose development was ahead of hers. Mainstream classes would be larger, true, but she would have a Special Needs Assistant.

Our thoughts were beginning to settle, but a nagging thought disturbed me. From her earliest days my mental picture, at positive times, had been of Heidi going to our local school with the others. I wanted her to be normal, not bussing off to a special school halfway across the city. Was I really focused on fulfilling Heidi's needs, or was I rationalizing the pros and cons in order to fulfil mine?

'...her lovely sunny personality and sense of humour'

We needed some external input. We found various articles and research studies on inclusion of children with DS and were pleased to find that their conclusions were the same as ours. The evidence of two major UK research studies seemed conclusive: children in mainstream schools performed better in all the measured attainment criteria. Differing abilities at the outset were allowed for in the studies. This settled our minds and we put Heidi forward for a place at the enhanced nursery. For her first year at school she would need a Statement of Special Educational Needs prepared by the Education Service. Our aim was that this would recommend Heidi for a place at our local mainstream school. I was heartened to find the school extremely positive about having her.

As usual, Heidi was very excited at the prospect of a new experience. She settled into the nursery immediately, enthusiastically joining in with everything (except waiting for her turn); watching and copying when she didn't know what to do.

There were complications, of course, mostly to do with her size. She was still tiny; on the DS height chart her best ever effort was the third centile. This means that, out of a hundred children with DS her age, she would be among the smallest three. So, she couldn't reach most of the activities at the nursery; her physiotherapist had to send in a special chair and stool to enable her to participate. Another side effect of her smallness is shown by this comment

from her first report: 'Heidi is very popular with all the children and she has to be rescued from those who are delighted to put her to bed all day.'

Our favourite remark in her report was this: 'Heidi's special strength must be her lovely sunny personality and sense of humour.' As we considered the next stage in her life, we hoped that this defining aspect of her character would continue to flourish. We prayed that it would not be stunted by a growing awareness of her disabilities, or through experiencing cruelty from others.

A Statement of intent

 The next stage was school, and by March the dreaded Statementing process was beginning. The Statement would consist of a detailed description of Heidi's special educational needs, and an equally specific list of the special educational provisions and staffing skills necessary to meet them. It would also describe any non-educational needs such as health problems. It would contain recommendations as to school placement and any extra arrangements required to meet Heidi's non-educational needs.

In order to prepare this document, reports were required from Heidi's nursery, paediatrician, speech therapist, physiotherapist, audiologist, educational psychologist and us. This necessitated endless meetings and assessments. Inevitably, not all the reports were submitted by the deadline; some were a month late. Despite my chivvying, the delay was passed down the line and the

Statement was not produced on time. My concern was that Heidi's Special Needs Assistant would not be appointed in time. The school could not appoint the position until the official confirmation came in the Statement. It would be horrible if Heidi could not start school with the other children simply because she had no assistant.

It seems a common experience that parents of children with special needs learn to be pushy on their behalf. Steve says that that comes more easily to some than to others. I'm not sure I know what he means by that! Anyway, after I sent off an angry fax, the draft Statement appeared with remarkable speed. We were thankful to find that we were happy with it and did not need to request any amendments. Unfortunately, it was still too late for the school to advertise the post of assistant, so we spent the summer hoping that they would be able to make an interim arrangement. Despite this loose end, it was a huge relief to come to the end of a long, hard struggle.

But other parents we knew or heard about were having a far tougher time than we had. Some schools were still very unwilling to take such children when it came to it, whatever their prospectuses might say. Some education authorities were far less pro-integration than ours. In God's plan our local authority had been criticized a few years before by a government report on its approach to integration. The result was that it now has one of the highest levels of integration in the country.

So, even if this was just a lull before the beginning of the next long, hard struggle, there were good reasons to be thankful for progress so far and to be encouraged as we contemplated the future.

We had wondered if this day would ever arrive. Heidi had fought her way through quite a few stages of her personal assault course to reach this momentous point: those first few months, when she was too concerned with merely staying alive to make any developmental progress; the repeated bouts of pneumonia over her first winter; her painstaking struggle to make up for that lost opportunity, all the while dragged back by the ball and chain of her physical and mental impairments.

After becoming lost several times in the maze of the Statementing process, we could at last see the 'EXIT' sign looming. The school was happy to welcome her for the beginning of term, although her assistant had not yet been appointed.

An interesting reception

So there she was, resplendent in her school uniform, just the same as the boys'. 'Room to grow' was putting it kindly, but she was so proud. It was quite a struggle to get her to sit still long enough to take the obligatory first-day photo, but there was no need to say 'cheese'. A huge grin was fixed more firmly on her face than the contortion you get on your wedding day.

Will she be all right? She seems so tiny in her uniform, not big enough for school. She's only just four. Will she cope? I hope they've got a temporary assistant organized for her.

The moment of truth arrived. I didn't want to let go of her hand, but Heidi didn't share my apprehensions. She pulled herself away and bounded in delightedly to meet her new friends. I was relieved to discover a Special Educational Needs Assistant in place. I recognized her as a fellow parent. 'Come in and tell me a bit about Heidi,' she said. I didn't want to tell her too much for fear that she would become a very temporary assistant. As we chatted, Heidi was becoming acquainted with her new environment: washing the sleeves of her pristine jumper in the water play area and checking out the sand to see if it tasted any better than the stuff at home. I realized from her reaction that Debbie Hemming was not going to be fazed by Heidi's idiosyncrasies.

Thankfully Mrs Hemming was going to fill in on a regular basis until the creaking wheels of Local Education Authority bureaucracy had completed their rotation and a permanent appointment was made. We had been concerned that it would be unsettling for Heidi to be continually having different helpers, or, worse still, none at all. We soon discovered that Mrs Hemming was the ideal assistant: enthusiastic, loving and firm. We hoped she would apply for the permanent job and were delighted when she was eventually appointed. The school's Special Educational Needs Co-ordinator, Karen Fenlon, was Heidi's class teacher, so we could not have wanted a better team.

Heidi quickly adapted to her new routine. She has never been fazed by change, taking great pleasure in each new experience. Because of her small stature and heart condition she still tired easily, so she only went to school in the mornings. We need not have been concerned that this would prevent her becoming a fully paid-up member of the class. She became extremely popular, although some of her classmates had to be dissuaded from treating her like a living doll. She soon seemed to know the name of nearly everyone in the school.

'Good mornin', Ryan. Good mornin', Emily.' It was a long haul to cross the playground each morning, like being on walkabout with the Queen.

She kept being stopped by the children for a conversation as she walked along the corridor or sat in the library doing one-to-one work with Mrs Hemming. This was creating so many distractions from her work that the children had to be asked to stop doing it.

'Just treat her like any other child.' It was a good aim and one which has gradually been achieved, but many of the children have a special affection for her. Even grunting, uncooperative eleven-year-old boys were transformed into angels of mercy in her presence. 'Come on, Heidi, take a penalty!' Never mind the fact that she would need at least ten kicks to reach the goal, the lads were determined that she should have a go. 'Well done, Heidi, brilliant goal!' Inevitably the goalkeeper had contrived to miss completely with his exaggerated attempt at a save. Heidi revelled in the celebrations and attention.

The penalty competition was part of a charity fund-raising event at the school.

As usual, Heidi was taking maximum enjoyment from the occasion. As soon as we had got through the gate, a swarm of chaperones had descended to remove her from us and escort her around the stalls.

'Heidi, here you are, I bought this for you.' *Marvellous, yet another teddy for our collection.*

'Heidi, have a go at the table football.' Not only did she win her match, but she won the whole competition. The test-match cricket authorities would have been appalled at such blatant match fixing, but she walked away with the prize without so much as an internal inquiry.

Her class's performance of *Goldilocks and the Three Bears* was one of her first opportunities to tread the boards. Predictably, she was not exactly overcome with stage fright. She was a flower but was not going to be content with a non-speaking part. Noticing the approval of the audience when she continued her dance after the other flowers had stepped down, she took every opportunity to add her own ad-hoc contributions to the script.

'Who's been eating my porridge?'

'It was her!' yelled Heidi, rushing onto the stage and pointing an accusing finger at Goldilocks.

The procession out at the end took rather longer than normal because she had to shake hands or touch the knees of most of the parents sitting by the aisle.

A number of the children and mums came up to me afterwards.

'Your little girl was the star of the show.' 'Isn't Heidi coming on well?' 'She brought the house down.' 'I'm so glad she's come here—it's really good for the school.' 'Mixing kids with Down's syndrome in mainstream schools is a great idea.'

Transgressing and progressing

Heidi's contributions did not always go down this well. When two boys were sent out of assembly for talking, she shouted out, 'Shh, shh, go to your classrooms!' Then, more quietly at intervals throughout the rest of the assembly, 'I'm a good girl, I am.'

'It's not funny is it, Heidi?'

Eventually Heidi learned to sit still and quiet with the other children. One day she proudly brought home her first certificate of achievement, for 'Sitting still and listening in assembly'. However, her assertions of goodness were not always backed up by her behaviour in class. When I went to pick up Heidi, I would usually be forewarned by two or three children before being approached by a solemn Miss Fenlon or Mrs Hemming to be told of the day's misdemeanours.

'I found Heidi with both hands down the toilet and toilet paper all over the floor.' Mrs Hemming's face was severe, but Heidi was standing beside her, head cocked to one side, looking up at her with a big grin. I struggled to keep my face straight.

'It's not funny is it, Heidi?' Mrs Hemming was saying.

'Yes, it is.'

'You won't do it again, will you?'

'Yes.' This was probably true, but not the best answer. Suzie would watch these exchanges and absorb them with great interest.

'Heidi was a very naughty girl at school today,' she would say at dinner time, and with great relish she would regale Steve with all the details.

It was slow going, but gradually Heidi realized that we and her teachers were not going to let her get away with hair-pulling or eating various unmentionable substances or pushing her classmates. Immature forms of behaviour such as these are a part of her delayed development, but she is perfectly capable of learning to behave in acceptable ways. It would be failing her if we let them pass with an apologetic: 'It's because she's got Down's syndrome', and we were pleased to find that her teachers shared our philosophy.

With so much stimulation her speech came on well, with longer and more complex sentences. Heidi started including more linking words. She hadn't bothered with them before because she could make herself understood without them. Alongside books from a reading scheme she was given key words on flash cards. By the end of her first term she could recognize about thirty-five words when she was in the mood. She would proudly bring her reading books home to show us. Suzie was very interested and would ask Heidi what the words said. It delighted Heidi to be of superior knowledge and teach them to her sister, and that delighted us.

The rest of the class were, of course, on a steeper learning curve. We were so pleased with her progress that it was easy to forget that she was learning much more slowly than the others. It was a jolting reminder to look around the classroom on parents' evenings and see the evidence staring down from the walls. It cheered us up to discover that she could read more words than some of her classmates, so at least she was keeping up in one area, so far. We feared that even this would not last much longer.

After the novelty of reading had worn off, Heidi would sometimes be lazy and claim not to be able to read her books. On one occasion she tripped herself up. Pointing to the next word, she said: 'I don't know that word "and"'!

Her first year soon drew towards its close, and Sports Day arrived. Heidi thoroughly enjoyed taking part in each activity. She is one of the few people who still subscribe to the dog-eared dictum 'It's not winning, it's taking part that counts.' It's a good thing she does or life would soon become depressing for her. My abiding image of that summer afternoon is of Heidi determinedly heading for the finishing line long after the other competitors had finished, face lit by a smile of pure joy. The children lining the track were clapping and shouting 'Hei-DI, Hei-DI' as she came in—a victor.

Reporting back

 'Although Heidi only scored at the first percentile, (ninety-nine per cent of same-age peers would perform better than Heidi did on this occasion) she has made progress.'

The cold combination of raw statistics and standard-format wording in the speech therapy end-of-term review gave us a jolt of dismay. We felt that she had been making good progress over her first school year; we had seen her developing. We felt the review, based on one twenty-minute snapshot when Heidi had a bad cold, did not do her justice, but the stark picture given was still a discouragement. We had no such problems with her school report:

'Heidi will spell her name correctly using magnetic letters ... enthusiastic ... excellent progress with her reading ... enthusiastic ... can count a set of ten objects with support ... enthusiastic ... come on in leaps and bounds ... enthusiastic ... delightful girl.'

Even the comments which could have been negative were couched in the wonderful language of Teacherese: 'She will sit still and listen for short periods of time, depending on how interested she is in the stimulus on offer.' Interpretation: After about thirty seconds she gets up and wanders off.

'She understands the importance of listening to others and is beginning to do this more frequently.' Interpretation: She still usually prefers talking.

'Heidi has a natural curiosity for her immediate environment and has enjoyed investigating and exploring within it.' Interpretation: She will immediately spot and grab anything messy and shove it in her mouth/ears/hair.

'She is beginning to develop more of a spatial awareness and is becoming more responsive to simple instructions.' Interpretation: She is not quite as clumsy as she was and occasionally does as she is told.

End of term: time to reflect on the year. There had been so many concerns and unknowns at the outset. Would our tiny tot be able to cope with 'big school'? Would she be picked on or laughed at? Would her placement in a group of mainstream-ability children just throw her limitations into depressingly sharp focus? Integration is not always successful. We knew of another mainstream school where a boy with special needs faced the possibility of being uprooted. 'We want to make a success of it,' his teacher and assistant would say, but they seemed unwilling to make that extra effort required.

Despite the initial pangs of anxiety, we had been convinced that integration was the best solution for Heidi. Our conviction had strengthened further during the year as we had observed her progress. We could look back with satisfaction, but it hadn't just 'happened'. The school had been wholly positive from the outset. Karen Fenlon and Debbie Hemming had been totally committed to Heidi and determined to do everything they could for her. These were essential ingredients for which we were deeply thankful.

But what of the rest of the school? How many people with Down's syndrome and other disabilities have suffered at the hands or tongues of people who do not have to live with their disadvantages? And how many of these incidences of prejudice are due to ignorance? Three hundred or so children had experienced Heidi that year. The vast majority had grown to appreciate her sameness and her difference. Surely those children who had laughed at her show-off stage performances and showered her with a seemingly endless stream of Christmas cards would not now grow up with hearts and minds closed to people like Heidi. They would be far more likely to accept and respect people for who they are, because ignorance had been overcome.

So now we could look back with great thankfulness on many fears allayed and countless prayers answered. Yes, there had been sad moments, but many happy, fulfilling hours. Our caring Father was still looking after his Heidi.

Chapter 9

Big little sister

 'Hello, what's your name?' We were back at the doctor's surgery and Heidi was making herself known in the waiting room. These visits were frequent, but never monotonous.

'Can you speak French?' On our holiday soon after her sixth birthday Heidi had become fascinated with the language.

'No, I can't.'

'I can. Un, deux, trois, quatre, cinq, six, sept, huit, neuf, dix.'

'I wish I could do that,' replied the lady, suitably impressed.

'Yes.' Then she was off again: 'Un, deux, trois ...'

'I only wish she'd learnt to count in English so quickly,' I said to the lady. It was a heartfelt comment; the process had seemed interminable. The thought took me back to one of those saddening moments when reality strikes home.

'Come on, Heidi, count with me: one, two ...'

'Four, eight, six, five,' Heidi joined in with great confidence.

'No, let's try again. One, two ...'

'Nine, three, seven, six ...' She had known the numbers for months. Why couldn't she count properly? I took a deep breath.

'Let's try again, Heidi. One, two ...'

'One, two, three, four, five, six, seven, eight, nine, ten' carolled a cheerful little voice. I looked up in surprise at Suzie's grinning face framed in the doorway. She was just starting to learn numbers. Only a day or two earlier she could only count to three.

The scenario was one which had been casting its lengthening shadow over us for some time. There was a grim inevitability about it, like that date with the dentist gleefully circled in red on the calendar by one's wife! For the previous six months or so the two of them had been broadly comparable: Heidi ahead with reading, writing and numbers; Suzie much quicker and more co-ordinated physically, and with clearer speech. But now Suzie was three and a quarter and loving the nursery she had just started. Numbers were swiftly mastered and, before long, letters would follow.

We had been delighted when Heidi had started to write her name during her previous school year. After much effort and practice she had learned the 'H'. 'I' and 'd' had followed eventually, but 'e' seemed beyond her. She would just leave gaps for someone else to fill them in. Now, some months later, 'e' still seemed an insurmountable obstacle.

One day Suzie announced, 'I want to write my name.' Half an hour later she had got it, Heidi's nemesis 'e' having been vanquished without a murmur. We had become so conditioned by constant repetition and reinforcement with Heidi that we had forgotten how easily and naturally a typical child picks things up.

It is a strange experience to be sad when your child makes progress. Yes, it is mixed with pleasure and pride, but it is sometimes an effort to be enthusiastic when it throws Heidi's limitations into such sharp relief. It is, of course, an effort that has to be made, to avoid being unfair to Suzie. But the unalloyed pleasure such achievements brought with the boys was missing as Suzie increasingly overtook Heidi in so many areas, with the effortlessness of a Ferrari powering past a dawdling truck.

 By this time Suzie had a definite height advantage too, although Heidi was still a division or two up in the weight department. For the previous year or so they had always been taken for twins by strangers. The response 'No, this one's three and that one's five' was usually met with the sort of look which said, 'There's either something wrong with my ears or your brain, and I think it's the latter.' It always gave me a pang of sadness; another sign of Heidi's 'big sister'-hood being denied by her Down's syndrome. But the subsequent explanation sometimes led on to further conversation. People would be amazed to hear what Heidi had been through, giving us a natural opportunity to share our faith: 'So many people were praying for her through that time. We're quite sure that God answered those prayers, because only he could have healed her.'

Heidi and Suzie are great friends

Suzie was not slow to make the most of this new-found opportunity to score points.

'I'm big and you're small, Heidi.'

'No, I'm big and you're small, Suzie.'

In an effort to bring some sense into this oft-rehearsed futility, I said one day, 'God made everyone different, girls. Some people are big and some are small.'

So next time Suzie opened with the pious gambit:

'God made me big and you small, Heidi.' It doesn't take a Kasparov to work out how the game continued, but Heidi wasn't going to concede without a fight.

On a school outing a couple of days later she was in an unfamiliar toilet.

'Careful when you get down, it's rather high,' warned Mrs Hemming.

'It's all right,' replied Heidi calmly from her precarious perch. 'God made me big.'

Heidi and Suzie are great friends and mostly play very well together. Their constant communication and imaginative games have certainly brought Heidi on in her development. But sometimes Suzie's bossiness is a bit hard to take. She soon noticed that we would praise Heidi for doing things that she herself could achieve quite easily. She decided that she would help with Heidi's education.

'Here you are, Heidi, can you put your socks on?' An excessive round of applause would ensue when Heidi good-naturedly obliged.

'Well done, Heidi, good girl. You ARE clever.' Unbeknown to Suzie, this was all said in the most patronizing tone imaginable. One time in the car I was severely reprimanded for failing to clap Heidi for some unspectacular achievement. Knowing Suzie, she would otherwise have torn me off a strip for removing my hands from the steering wheel.

Next, Suzie moved on to correcting Heidi's pronunciation errors, real or imagined. Heidi had problems with some sounds, pronouncing 'l' like 'y' and 'r' like 'w'. She could say 's' clearly, but at this time was missing it off the beginning of words. This lazy habit had to be corrected by constant reminders to pronounce the words properly. Suzie took this a stage further by deliberately making her say appropriate words.

'What's this, Heidi?' dangling a toy before her eyes.

'It's a 'nake.'

'No, Heidi, SSnake. Say SSnake, Heidi.'

'SSSnake,' said Heidi obligingly.

She didn't seem to mind, but I was offended for her dignity. All at once I felt miserable and jealous. Jealous of one daughter on behalf of the other. Jealous of all those other families who just have typical children.

It was a longstanding struggle. My mind rewound once more to that moment in the hospital five years before when I had held baby William, my envy drained. Yes, it had been a real and powerful answer to my prayers. But if I had thought my problem was over, I was soon disillusioned. I had not been immunized against jealousy. My weakness is ongoing and has resurfaced at regular intervals.

'Hello, Liz, how are you? Have you heard the news? Alison's had a baby girl!'

'Oh, how lovely!' My mouth asked the appropriate questions, but behind the plastic smile I was suddenly spinning again. *Why wasn't my baby normal? It's not fair! Another perfect baby at church. And it had to be a girl, didn't it?*

The strength of my reaction took me by surprise. Heidi was nine months old then, and I had thought I was getting past this sort of thing. *Haven't I really accepted her after all?*

Thankfully I haven't had such strong feelings when babies have been born since, although it still brings a twinge sometimes. But, to my shame and sadness, the right triggers can still set off an explosion.

'Now, Heidi, you're all dressed again in clean, dry clothes. If you need the potty, tell me.' My voice was still calm, but my frustration was growing as high as the pile of wet clothes.

'Yes, mummy,' Heidi agreed cheerfully, as though I was telling her something very obvious. Week after week this had gone on, and today was worse than ever. *She's three years old; why can't she get it? Will she ever get it?*

'Mummy, I need the potty.' She was stepping gingerly towards me, legs bowed as if she'd just dismounted after a long ride. The dark patch on her trousers was an unnecessary confirmation. *Down's syndrome. It wrecks everything!*

Growing pains

'We think it would be better for Heidi to go back into the Reception class again,' the teacher was saying. Heidi had gone up with her class at the end of her first year. I had been so pleased at the review when this had been decided. Someone had said that the class would be incomplete without her.

'She is already spending quite a lot of time with the Reception class, and making good progress. She can't really do group work with the Year One class because of the gap in ability.' I had known it was coming but it didn't make it feel any better. The tears flooded when I told Steve. He did his best to cheer me up:

'She's only a couple of months older than some of the Reception children anyway, and if she's going to go down a year, it's better now than later. If she's there a lot anyway, it will be more settled to be part of the class. She'll make better progress if she can work in groups with the other children.'

Great, the voice of reason telling me what I already know. Thanks a lot. Why does she have to have Down's syndrome?

When I'm exhausted after a difficult day; when Heidi's limitations are shown up in comparison with another child; when she can't or won't do something that I feel she should be able to do; when I stop relying on God: that's when it happens. I stamp my metaphorical foot and shake my little fist at God. *It's not fair! I don't want her to have Down's syndrome any more. Why can't she be NORMAL?*

It is a struggle from which I know I will never be free. For all her lovableness and rich character, Heidi will always have a disability. It will prevent her from doing and being some things. My challenge is to conquer those moments when my sadness turns against the God who has given us such a beautiful, different, gift.

Secondary thoughts

She stood proudly in her tiny uniform, hands hiding in the sleeves, trousers almost brushing the ground. Just about all I could see of her was a huge grin and sparkling eyes … hang on, haven't I written something like this before? Yes, of course, it was all very familiar, though all so new. This time Heidi was looking forward excitedly to another session at her new school. Hopefully, after having experienced plenty of these trial days, the huge school full of massive girls would not be too daunting when she moved there in September. We found that the local mainstream girls' secondary school was very keen for Heidi to go there, despite her being thirteen when she would start, two school years older than everyone else. The special needs co-ordinator was amazingly helpful in what she was willing to do to accommodate Heidi's needs.

As Heidi approached this new chapter in her life, we could look back over the years since she first started school and see so many changes. Yet we could also recognize some familiar themes. Some of these recurring experiences try our limited patience and wisdom; others bring us joy and blessing. But there is one unchanging truth, God's faithfulness, constantly exemplified in living three-dimensional reality, which gives us security for the present and hope for the future.

Gluten free time

It was time again for a measuring session. One by one the children stood against the height chart stuck to the door and keenly checked how much progress had been made in the last six months. When it was Heidi's turn one of us had to hold her feet down to stop her standing on tiptoes, and another had to keep her head still, or she would stick her chin in the air to try to sneak a few extra millimetres. Finally we got enough steadiness to make a mark on the chart.

'Have I grown, have I grown?' she squealed, jumping up and down.

'Er, yes, Heidi, half a centimetre.'

'YESSS!' she shouted, delighted at this result. Maths is still not her best subject.

Unfortunately, this was a typical rate of progress; she was still only the size of a six-year-old at the age of eleven. I mentioned this to the GP and Heidi was referred to a paediatrician. After various tests it was established that she had coeliac disease. An intolerance of gluten meant that she was not absorbing her food properly. One of the signs is failure to grow. Although it was good to have the potential for growth, the downside was that she would have to go on a strict gluten-free diet. Since gluten is in wheat and is also added to many processed foods as a binding agent, this would be quite difficult for her. Would she understand that she wouldn't be allowed to eat normal bread, cakes, pizzas and pasta, and that there were many cereals, sweets and ice creams she couldn't have? And once the damaged villi in her gut had healed, even a small amount of gluten could cause a bad reaction and undo a lot of good.

Why does she have to have yet another thing wrong with her? Down's syndrome, leukaemia, pneumonia, open heart surgery, ongoing struggles with learning and practical skills and now coeliac disease —hasn't she got enough problems? I certainly feel like I have. We approached the start of the diet with prayer and trepidation.

We weren't encouraged when we sampled the gluten-free products she would have to eat—to the rest of us they were mostly dry and unpalatable. Thankfully Heidi was bringing to this situation her usual positive approach to life with its changes and new experiences. She was looking forward to her special diet and proclaimed the bread, rolls and cakes to be delicious. The other children helped too, although that sometimes led them into slightly tricky situations:

'Oh, PLEASE can I have one of Heidi's special cakes?' accompanied by vigorous headshaking and gagging impressions out of Heidi's line of sight.

'No, Tim, they are for Heidi,' I replied, as expected. Unfortunately, Tim hadn't reckoned with Heidi's generous spirit. She insisted he had one and was not to be put off. She keenly watched him eat it.

'Do you like it, Tim?'

'They're nice for you, aren't they?'

'Yes, but do you like it?'

'It's the best gluten-free cake I've ever had' (muttering the 'gluten-free' under his breath).

'Yes, but do you like it?'

'Er ...' Then inspiration struck: 'I think it's outstanding in its field.' Thankfully this was taken as a yes, and Tim was off the hook.

A major concern was whether Heidi would be able to take on board the importance of her diet. While she was at home we could keep a close eye on what she was eating, but would she remember when she was at school or at a friend's house? If everyone else was having one of her favourite chocolate biscuits, it would be very hard for her to resist the temptation to have one.

We were very thankful that she embraced the necessary legalistic approach with amazing maturity; another answer to prayer.

'Am I allowed it?'

'I won't give you anything you aren't allowed, will I?'

'I'm going to check the ingredients. Glucose syrup, cocoa butter, crisped rice, modified starch … yes, I'm allowed that.'

The constant questioning sometimes tries our patience, especially when it comes to insisting on checking the list of ingredients on a pack of pure orange juice, for example. But Heidi's cheerful acceptance of this imposition on her is a chastening example to the rest of the family, with our tendency to be easily irritated over small things. As the novelty has worn off, she occasionally makes comments like 'I wish I could have that chocolate fudge cake' or 'I'll have coeliac disease for the rest of my life, won't I?' but she never complains or feels sorry for herself.

 Like peering into the distance on a foggy day, we are tempted to stare too hard into the future, as if that will make the misty shadows take on a form. But that mistake only scares us; we need to focus on what is just in front of us. When Heidi talks about her ambitions for the future, it sometimes saddens us, as we wonder whether she will achieve them.

'Daddy, can you do my buttons up, please?'

'Can't you do these ones?'

'No.'

'Tell you what, just have a go while I sort Suzie out.'

I returned some minutes later, sorting Suzie out having taken much longer than anticipated, to find Heidi struggling patiently with the second button.

'How are you getting on?'

'Quite well, thanks,' she replied cheerfully.

'Keep practising,' I said, while I did up the rest of the buttons, 'and you'll get the hang of it. You can't go through your whole life asking people to do your buttons up, can you?'

'Why not?' she asked, puzzled.

'It would be a bit strange when you were grown up, wouldn't it?'

'Oh yes, it would be weird when you were an adult to ask your husband to do your buttons up,' she giggled.

The sharp juxtaposition of her ongoing limitations and her clear anticipation of her future gave me a sudden pang.

Moments like these are one of the things that haven't changed. It's one of those familiar themes, along with health concerns, developmental issues, Heidi's ability to touch people's hearts, and times when the family is dissolved into helpless laughter at one of Heidi's ridiculous remarks. But the most important unchanging fact is God's goodness to Heidi, which we know, and she knows, will continue for the rest of her life. Because of this Heidi doesn't worry about the future, and we don't need to either. If the future doesn't turn out as she anticipates, she will take it in her short but determined stride, because her firm trust is in her God.

Cold feet

 'Hi, Liz, it's Stella from the Down's group. A girl's just had a positive amnio and she'd like to speak to someone. She's called Tracey. She's only twenty-one. Would you go and see her?'

The sinking feeling came on as soon as I'd put the phone down. I'd volunteered to talk to new or prospective parents of babies with DS. It had seemed a good idea at the time, a useful way to use my experience and hopefully help others. Now it came to it, my feet were getting decidedly chilly. *She's only just had the amniocentesis test result. She might not have decided whether to keep the baby yet.* Since the baby was labelled 'substandard', it was legal to have an abortion right up to birth. *What if she's waiting to see me before she makes up her mind? I'd feel terrible if she decided to have an abortion after I had spoken to her.*

I tipped my worries out onto Steve.

'You can't make it sound like a bed of roses; just tell it like it is. Whatever happens, you mustn't feel guilty. It's her decision and her responsibility.'

I wonder how she's feeling. The grief, the tears, the heartache: back they came. Fresh and crisp out of cold storage, the emotions washed through me anew. It was exhausting to go through it again. I spent a night dreaming about babies with Down's syndrome being expected or born. I would be glad when it was over. I hoped Tracey wasn't thinking the same.

We told the boys about it at Bible Time so they too could pray about my visit.

'That's great—another baby with DS!' was their immediate response.

'I could tell her what you think it's like having a sister with DS'

This was eight-year-old Daniel's verdict:

'She's priceless. I wouldn't swap her for anyone, because she's so funny and because she's my sister. Although she's had a very troubled little life, she's my sister and that's all that matters.'

Tim's answers were equally positive. He also asked me to tell Tracey about God, because he was sure it would help her.

The day came and once again my anxieties proved wasted energy. Tracey was very positive and there seemed to have been no thought of having an abortion.

'Thank you, Lord,' I said as I mulled my visit over on the way home. More prayers answered. *I hope I haven't depressed her by mentioning some negative things … here we go again. When will I learn to stop worrying?*

The boys were very keen to find out how I had got on.

'Did you tell her about God?' Tim asked immediately.

'Er, no.'

'Why not?' His face betrayed his shock and disappointment.

'There didn't seem to be a suitable moment,' I replied lamely.

'Then you'll have to go back again and tell her.'

The issue was so clear to him; no unnecessary complications. Stung by my failure, I wished I could be more like that. Surely that is part of what Jesus meant when he said, 'Be like little children.'

Big little sister

Chapter 10

Amazing grace

 Heidi's bedtime was usually a pleasure. There was the pleasant consequence of peace for the rest of the evening, but it was also a tonic in itself. A big hug, a slobbery kiss, sometimes a comment like: 'I love you, you're the best daddy in the world'. It was enough to ease the strain if the evening with the children had been fractious. She was generally happy to go to bed; although when she had some idea about telling the time we occasionally had a disagreement.

'Heidi, time to go up to bed.'

'No, my bedtime is quarter to eight.'

'But it's five to eight now.'

'So, it's not my bedtime then!'

Fortunately, she soon mastered the concept of earlier and later; but once we convinced her that she wasn't being conned, she went off quite amicably. Heidi took great delight in the goodnight process, particularly doing her Bible notes. Her prayers became thoughtful, and she remembered lots of needs which had been mentioned at home or church. A few years before, they tended to veer from the ridiculous to the sublime.

'Please help Suzanna to stop makin' that racket in her bedroom. It's giving me an 'eadache.' Heidi had no problem with the concept of nothing being too small to pray about. Another time, she turned to me after her prayer and said, 'I was praying to God, wasn't I? I like God. He's a nice chap.' Not theologically profound, but a little sign of a growing appreciation of important truths.

Heidi had always been very keen to take her turn to say grace before meals. We sometimes had to remind the others to think about what they were saying and come up with something more original than a mechanical 'Dear God, thank you for this lovely food. Amen'. But this had never been necessary with

Heidi, as she always had plenty of things to thank God for or tell him about. At times, the dinner went cold by the time she had finished; but that was a small price to pay.

One day, when she was about five and a half, her growing understanding crystallized into this prayer:

'Thank you for this food we have here. Help us to trust in God and Jesus. Thank you that Jesus died on the cross for our sins. Amen.'

Liz dissolved into tears of pure joy, and we thanked God for the simple truths of his gospel.

Soon after this we were going through a book of 'Questions and Answers' at Bible Times.

'Suzie, what was the most important thing Jesus came to do?' Suzie put on the coy look which would no doubt be put to good use in future years.

'I don't know,' she whimpered helplessly.

'Died on the cross,' put in Heidi. 'To save us from our sins.'

'Well done, Heidi,' Liz enthused. 'There's a verse to learn too. "Jesus came into the world to save sinners." Can you say that, Suzie?'

Once more Suzie wasn't up to the task, but Heidi repeated it perfectly. We secretly relished the increasingly rare opportunity for Heidi to outshine Suzie. More deeply, we appreciated Heidi's unaffected enthusiasm for the truths at the heart of the Bible.

Yes, some parts of the Bible are hard to understand. But even people such as Heidi, or indeed with far more severe learning difficulties, can understand enough to be sure of the good news in Jesus. Nor should we assume that they will just be hangers-on in God's kingdom.

Heidi may not become a great scientist or strut across the world's political stage, but if she knows God, she will bring him glory in her life and enjoy his presence for ever. Her legacy may be far more worthwhile than that of many illustrious achievers who have no knowledge of the true God.

Although Heidi's physical growth had been painfully slow, it was a joy to see her grow spiritually. Reading her Bible and Bible notes at bedtime often became the highlight of her day. She absorbed it all with great enthusiasm and often quoted things she has remembered a long time later. We realized that she would be able to read and understand the notes on her own and suggested she might like to do an extra one in the morning sometimes. The next day she had completed a week's worth of Psalms before anyone else had woken up!

Heidi loved Sundays. She was keen to go to the prayer meeting before the morning service and joined in with at least one prayer of her own. During sermons she often wrote her own prayers and songs, which revealed her understanding of Bible truth and her love for God. Often she appeared to be paying no attention to the sermon, but suddenly whispered loudly 'What does "propitiation" mean?' or whatever it might be. And lunchtime conversations often revealed that she had taken in a lot.

Heidi loves to write her testimony. We have a number of versions, all written in Heidi's unique and rather random style. Like varieties of rose, they are all different, yet all beautifully the same.

It is striking that Heidi seems more able when engaged in Christian activity. As Pastor Paul explained it: 'Heidi is probably the only person in the church who is more advanced spiritually than naturally.' By nine she could read fluently. When she read a story book, she would not always read with understanding and was quite happy to gloss over it and press on. However, when it was a word she didn't understand in the Bible, she always stopped and asked. Heidi loves to sing, and knows an amazing number of songs and hymns. Once she started singing a hymn I didn't realize she knew at all:

Name of all majesty,
fathomless mystery,
King of the ages
by angels adored;
power and authority,
splendour and dignity,
bow to his mastery—
Jesus is Lord!

I was impressed that she knew the whole verse off by heart—and when she carried on straight through the remaining three verses I was amazed. This was a child who could not always remember what number comes after twelve;

it speaks powerfully of God's goodness to Heidi. It also demonstrates the truth that God is not limited in his ability to bring his grace into a person's heart. Where we may easily see a barrier of mental ability, culture, language, religion or whatever it might be, God may see a person whom he will choose to transform.

> ## My testimony
>
> He healed me when I had meuktoc mia. When I read my bibile I believed what it said. I really love him cause he died for me. He was really loving when he was washing my sins away.
>
> I love the bible because it is full of truth and respect. When I read it i believed it.
>
> Singing songs and praising Jesus is what i love to do. And i like telling people about Jesus 'Cause he is my best friend foRever.
>
> by Li heidi

Heidi's testimony at her baptism in June 2008

An enquiring mind!

'Mummy, how can God love the Pharisees?' the voice suddenly piped from the back of the car.

'God IS love, Heidi, it's just what he is like.' If I had thought I could get away with a nice simple answer, my hopes were soon dashed.

'I know that,' came the reply, rather impatiently. 'But they killed his Son. I just don't understand how he could love them.'

'We've all done lots of terrible things against God, but he still loves us, doesn't he?'

'Yes, I know, but how could he love the Pharisees? I just can't get my head round it.'

I gave up at this point and referred her a couple of branches up the theological tree (Dad) or else go straight to the top and ask Pastor Paul. Unfortunately, she didn't follow my advice. At the same point in the same journey the next day:

'Mummy, how can God love the Pharisees?' Pretty much the same conversation followed, with the same unconvinced Heidi at the end.

'Mummy, how can God love the Pharisees?' By the fourth time this was asked at the same point in the same journey I was beginning to wonder if it was Groundhog Day.

'Why don't you ask me a different question?'

'OK. Why did God hide his face from his Son when he was on the cross?'

I suppose I should have known better than to expect that another question would make things easier!

In this instance the questioning showed that Heidi's mind was enquiring and wrestling with spiritual questions, but it also illustrates her habit of repeating questions over and over again, or asking questions to which she knows the answer. When her Bible notes asked her to write down a bad habit that she would make a resolution to change. She wrote 'stop asking annoying questions', so we were quite hopeful.

'When are you coming up to put me to bed?' she called down the next evening, as usual.

'In a few minutes.'

'But when?'

'Heidi, you know what a resolution is, don't you?'

'Yes, but it's not New Year yet!'

An enquiring mind

Chapter 11

The bridge on the River Why?

 'The tiny little girl called Fiona Finger was very, very ill. She was just about to die when a good fairy flew down and touched her with her wand. Fiona opened her eyes and smiled. From that moment she grew stronger and stronger and grew into a happy child who brought much joy to her parents. But sometimes they were still sad because she was too small to do everything the other children did. One day her mummy had another baby girl. She soon grew into a big strong child with blonde hair and blue eyes. She loved her little sister Fiona and played with her all the time. Now their mummy and daddy were really happy and they all lived happily ever after.'

I closed the book carefully to avoid waking the sleeping child.

No, you're right, it's not even a real fairy story.

'Why?' was the question most often on our lips and in our minds. It lay before us unyielding, impenetrable. Slowly the question became easier. We had four healthy children and Heidi was delightfully alternative. We have all benefited from her difference; and so have many others. We have learnt a lot about God and ourselves and the value of life. And our story is by no means ended.

We know there are others who cannot look back from a happy vantage point. They may still be in the middle of the storm. Perhaps there are happy moments during the struggle, but there seems no prospect of coming out on the other side. The hard grind continues unceasing day after wearisome day. There are husbands and wives betrayed and abandoned by their partners. Parents, whose children have died or have rejected their parents' faith. Others have deep and secret pains—physical, mental, emotional or spiritual. Perhaps you are reading this book with incomprehension or anger. In your circumstances you can see no light at the end of the tunnel, no reason. So, how can you find light in the tunnel. When you can see no 'Because', how do you deal with the 'Why'?

Job, a character in the Bible, seemed to have it made. Plenty of money and possessions, a large happy family, good reputation, many friends. Then, suddenly, he lost it all. The man who had everything, had nothing. Wealth, happiness and reputation evaporated overnight. Was God punishing him for some wicked deed? No. Job feared God and hated evil. This was his reaction to the devastation of his life: 'The LORD gave and the LORD has taken away; may the name of the LORD be praised' (Job 1:21).

Added to all his tragedy, Job's whole body became covered with painful sores. Did he give up on God? No. His response was: 'Shall we accept good from God, and not trouble?' (Job 2:10).

Of course, Job struggled to cope with his miserable situation. At one point he wished he had never been born (Job 3:16). He couldn't understand why all this was happening to him and he poured out his frustration in torrents of questions to God. But he never let go of his faith in God. In the midst of such deep trouble, he still had the confidence to cry out: 'God knows the way that I take; when he has tested me, I shall come forth as gold' (Job 23:10). Whether the gold would appear in this life or the next, Job did not know. But he did know with unflinching certainty that God's plan would one day be seen to be right.

Healthy family, delightful Heidi, lessons learnt—yes, for us there is some truth in the answers to our 'Why? But often they are deeply inadequate. God has given us many good things, but if he should choose to take them away again are our 'answers' gone also?

'Steve! Come quickly! Heidi looks terrible.' I rushed upstairs. Heidi was lying in her bed, shivering uncontrollably. Her breathing was shallow, her pulse fast. She was purple all over, turning to blue at her fingers and toes. *Oh no, not this again.* Soon I was on my way to hospital with her. Once more my mind was projecting a series of graphic images onto a screen in my head. Tubes, heart failure, consultants, pneumonia, machinery, leukaemia, operation, oxygen, breathing. A jumbled-up rapid-fire summary of those terrible times. *Please, not again. She's only eight!*

When we arrived at the hospital Heidi had brightened up a lot and all the symptoms were fading. By the time the doctor saw her she was ready to play. I felt embarrassed and foolish as she laughed and chatted with the doctor—

Heidi was a picture of health.

I strapped her back into the car at midnight.

'We had great fun at the hostibal [sic], didn't we, mummy?' she grinned.

Emergencies like this have frequently come out of the blue. 'We still don't know what tomorrow holds'—or even today. But the suddenness with which Heidi's health can deteriorate is unnerving.

So many times during those dark, mystifying years we felt totally out of control—we were. Yet God was in complete control the whole time. From our perspective Heidi almost died any number of times. Her life was dangling by the merest of threads. But from God's viewpoint she was far safer than the gold in Fort Knox. There was no chance of her dying, because his time had not come. That will continue to be true for the rest of her life and ours. Nothing will surprise him, and his plan is perfect.

With Heidi, the future is even more uncertain than for most of us, not only from a health perspective but in many other ways. We always knew that one day she would no longer be a cute bundle of fun, and we could envisage many potential problems as she grows towards adulthood: independence, accommodation, work, social life, relationships, prejudice and health. And more unforeseen. Or, maybe God will take her back to himself—his creation whom he has loaned to us. Will we then start angrily asking 'Why?' again?

Job realized that ultimately the only answer lies in the character of God. What we have experienced over the turbulent years of Heidi's life has demonstrated this to be true. We deserve nothing from God who is the Creator and Ruler of the universe and a loving Father to all who trust him. The good that we enjoy, we do not deserve,

There may be nothing wrong in asking God why such a thing has happened to us. It is certainly better to express to him how we feel than to pretend we are not having such thoughts. But there is a world of difference between a perplexed yet submissive 'Why?', that is eager to learn what God is teaching us, and a foot-stamping, rebellious 'Why? It's not fair', that implies we deserve something better.

How has God responded to our often ungracious and ungrateful response to his surprise gift? By continuing to be gracious. He has given us the support of loving friends and family. He has provided excellent medical care. He has preserved Heidi's life. He has guided our decisions when we were at our wits' end. As we struggled to trust him, he continued to demonstrate his total trustworthiness. Although we quickly reach the end of our meagre resources, we have learnt that we can always depend on him.

This chapter began with a fairy tale, because it may have appeared that our story finishes with a 'happily ever after'. But this book is not a fairy story, and Heidi's story is not yet finished.

Chapter 12

My own story

 'Hi, my name is Heidi Carter—well, I was Heidi Crowter until 2020, but we'll come to that later—I am twenty-seven and I happen to have Down's syndrome.

You may ask: What is Down's syndrome?

Let me take you back to your science lessons when you learn about chromosomes, every human being has twenty-three pairs of chromosomes, making forty-six in all. But someone with DS has one extra which means we may learn slower and have some level of learning disability.

But that can't stop us from living vibrant, active lives and living life to the full. Some people think that we can't do things: we can't walk, talk, have a job or live independently. I can do many things, and one of the things I am very proud of is living on my own in my very own flat. I can cook beef crumble, lasagna, three cheese pasta and toad-in-the-hole. I have awesome 'Future Guides'— that's what we call those we employ to support us in our independent living.

Before Covid 19 I had a job which I adored doing, I worked in a kids hair salon, my role included social media, sweeping the floor, taking payments and keeping the children amused while they have their hair done.

I am a passionate follower of Jesus Christ my Lord and King of my life. The Bible doesn't say that only people with forty-six chromosomes are fearfully and wonderfully made. No, it says that everyone is fearfully and wonderfully made, including me with my forty-seventh chromosome!

I, Heidi Carter, will never keep silent, I will keep fighting so that people with DS are treated equally.

In my first year I survived heart failure, leukaemia, pneumonia and kidney failure. My mum and dad were warned lots of times that I would not survive. But God answered their prayers and twenty-seven years later I am still here. So, you can see I am a fighter! I love these words in the Bible:

'You created my inmost being; you knit me together in my mother's womb. I praise you because I am fearfully and wonderfully made' (Psalm 139:13,14)

My schools

I went to two mainstream schools had great fun and worked hard—some of the time! The first one was Mount Nod primary school. I went with my siblings, so I had people to turn to when I had any problems. I made a lot of friends who I still have on Facebook, and I had a support worker called Mrs Hemming; me and her got on like a house on fire. She worked with me from reception to Year 6. She needs a trophy for having me for so long! I did Reception twice and I did Year 2 twice because I learn slower than anyone else, but I enjoyed it and I had to work on my playing skills and communicate with people.

This was my beautiful cerise prom dress

I don't remember that much of primary school, but I really enjoyed it, and made quite a lot of friends. One memory I have was when I was having my lunch and my mum burst in and said, 'Heidi you forgot your lunch box'; I was embarrassed, I was thinking, 'Just give me my lunch and go!'

Then I went to Tile Hill Wood school and language college and gained GCSES and BTECS. The one I am most proud of is getting a C in Foundation French as that is the highest grade you can get for Foundation stage. I felt so proud about getting a C because it felt so overwhelming that I had finally done all the hard work and it all paid off. I also got a GCSE in RE. I did a BTEC in Home Cooking skills, which has helped me a lot, and ASDAN Maths and a BTEC in applied science. I also got a GCSE in English.

I had a dream school experience in both of my schools. I loved it and everyone absolutely loved me. I used to put on little concerts by the English block every break and lunch time. I would do different concerts and I would do different songs and people would walk by and say their requests.

Here is my blog introducing my Year 11 Prom in 2013.

Hey blog readers
On the 21st of June I had my Year 11 prom. I went with my buddy from Grapevine which is a club for young people with disabilities. Her name is called Jo. I wore a cerise pink dress, and I had my hair like Audrey Hepburn. When my mum walked in when it was done, she burst into tears because I looked so grown up…. The day came for me to shine, and my amazing sister did my makeup she was my makeup artist. The dress made me feel like Cinderella; I had some silver shoes on. The prom was held at the Hilton Hotel in Walsgrave…. We had a three-course meal. For the starter we had leak and potato soup; it was delicious. For the main course I had chicken in white wine sauce, even tastier than the starter. For dessert we had strawberries squeezed to a pulp; it was amazing. Then I got up and danced.

While I was in Year 10 I had a day release and went to Coventry and Warwickshire Chamber of Commerce Training and did a BTEC in Hairdressing and Beauty. I chose to do hairdressing as it's very creative for me and fits my personality. Then I went to Heart of England training and did another National Vocational Qualification (NVQ) in Hairdressing and I loved it. I also did an NVQ in Customer Services to get a job. I learnt about the issues that some people have and how to help them. I found out about the employment support service (TESS) who help people with special needs to get jobs.

Out to work

I met a lovely lady called Karen and we instantly made friends;I found out that her birthday is the same day as the Hollywood actress Angelina Jolie and my granny. We are still friends today, she got me a job in a children's hair salon in Leamington spa specialising in children with disabilities.

I worked there for four years and loved it because I love kids and I had the best boss ever! My role was the salon junior doing the reception duties, taking the payments, booking appointments, learning how to use the card machine. I also did all the stock take, amusing the kids, putting the DVD's on for them; if they were old enough I would read books to them. I just loved helping and playing with the kids, washing their hair and distracting them while they have their hair cut.

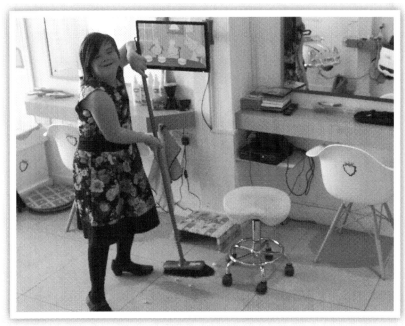

A salon junior's work is never done

Here I learned how to make conversation with people, listen to their answers and not to narrate what I am doing and just do it! Sadly, due to Covid I had to hand in my notice which was heart-breaking for me because I was saying goodbye to the best job I had.

But I have a new job now in devising drama sessions for kids with Down's syndrome. I help with drama workshops for kids of varying ages with DS; they are non-verbal workshops, which is quite trying for me as I like to talk! I would love to thank my sister Suzie for helping me in this job; she has taught me how to act professionally and I really feel that if I impress my colleagues it will lead to new opportunities.

I also work in a charity shop called the British Heart Foundation. My role includes, helping with the stock and labelling the DVD's and putting them on the shelves; I also welcome people and hold the donation bucket to collect donations for the charity.

I am a patron of a charity called *The Ups of Down's*, a fantastic organisation in North Leamington School and I help with their early development and speech therapy; I play with the children and talk to the parents and encourage them—I love it.

I am also a patron of a charity called *Positive about Down Syndrome* which aims to help families with kids with DS to live a life as happy and healthy like me and James. We had a day out with them, and we had lots of fun holding gorgeous babies with DS.

I received the Queen's award in the Girls Brigade which is the highest award that a girl can get. I had to learn about our British heritage and the laws that they make. I attended one of the Queen's garden parties and I loved It. I was a steward and I wore a nice dress. Unfortunately, I didn't see the Queen, but I had a great time meeting new people and finding out new birthdays.

I am an ambassador for *Mencap* which is a charity that produces 'Easy Read' for people with disabilities so they can understand what is written; they also campaign for rights for people with learning disabilities. I used their easy read manifestos to help me choose who to vote for in the General Election

I have worked with *Grapevine* which is an advocating charity for young people with and without disabilities. I have helped implement a Safe Places scheme in the city centre to help people with disabilities who are lost, scared or experiencing hate crime. If they see a Safe Place sticker in the shop, café or bank window, they can go in and the people will help them. I helped train people in how to help the person with disabilities. I also shared this scheme with the police and talked to them about how they can help people with disabilities. With *Grapevine* I worked on a University of Coventry research project about Education and Health Care Plans (EHCP), and how they are written and making sure that they are person-centred. We have interviewed professionals and offered them advice on how to help the EHCP process work better. We went to London to present our findings to the Government's Department of Education.

I have also lectured trainee nurses at Coventry University. I don't let anything stand in my way.

The skills I have learnt in my life

In life we all learn things every day. Since I was two, I started the skill of talking and I have never stopped since! I have also learnt that you don't wear brand new posh shoes to take out the rubbish—as you will discover later. I have also learnt the art of obeying your parents in everything. Sometimes I fail but I learn from my mistakes.

A skill I am still learning is fine motor skills; this is hard for me because my mum says I have fat fingers, which I agree with. For example, I was playing Chinese Checkers with my parents and I picked up one checker and because of fat fingers I dislodged the other ones. I have also learnt that when your baby sister is born you don't poke and prod her eyes out.

I am still learning how to speak clearly and slowly. One tool which is very helpful in slowing down your speech is to use your hand as you speak. As I use my hands, I feel that I am slowing down as my body is always in a rushing mood. I tend to rush things and do things slapdash; but I have learnt that rushing can lead to breaking things and if you rush things you will make mistakes and it will take longer. I have also learned a lot from my little sister Suzie. She has taught me how to behave like an adult, and we have fun as well.

I have also been taught how to eat like a lady! To be honest I am still working on my table manners. My mum says I eat like a pig at a trough, and I have to agree with her.

I have also learned the art of maturity, which is still a work in progress. Which means using your brain and thinking for yourself and not just relying on your parents, because if you rely on your parents you will get lazy and never learn stuff for yourself. We are always learning every day. I am still learning how to read people's body language, which shows if they are interested in what you are saying for example. And never speak to my mum about Football!

In my early years I learnt how to read. Now I can read anything. My favourite book to read is the Bible because it deepens my love for God, and you get to unpack the beautiful gift of my Lord Jesus Christ in all his splendour. One of the skills that I struggle with is patience, but the more I read the Bible the more I become like Jesus in his patience.

The gifts I am blessed with

I have a gift of finding the positive in every situation. It has been a thread throughout my life from since I was a child all through my teen years and into adulthood. I think it creates a good impact on people and my family has been fully blessed with my positive approach. I think it's very good to have a smile because it brightens people's days. My friend Karen wrote in my birthday card: 'Thank you for always brightening up my days.'

When Liverpool lose the champions league matches I say, 'Oh well at least we qualify for next year's champions league.' When we were in lockdown because of Covid 19 I didn't see it as lockdown, I saw it as quality family time. Once upon a time I hated monopoly, but when I won I changed my attitude towards the game and when I lose I say, 'I will try again next week.' I am also learning how to play chess which is quite tricky.

I always try to stay positive even when things are going wrong. The reason for this is that I am a strong Christian; that is my secret to keeping positive. I just look to heaven, and I smile that my Lord will come again and sort this world out. So how can I not be positive when the God who made me is coming again to judge the earth in righteousness. I rest in my Saviour's loving care and if I have Jesus on my side why should I be negative?

I am also blessed by God with a fantastic memory for the things I want to remember—my parents call it 'selective memory'! I have always loved finding out people's birthdays because I can always remember to phone them or send them a message, especially if it's someone who is older and lonely; it always cheers them up. The reason I do birthday cards is I am hoping that people who I send cards to will see the love and the care I show in writing them and will see Jesus in me. Some of my friends are a bit forgetful so I remind them that their family member has a birthday coming up soon!

I also have the skill of cheering people up when they are sad and down. I call them and pray with them, and sometimes send them cards to be the sunshine in their lives. At church there are people who have left their home countries as asylum seekers; it really cheers them up when I remember their birthdays. Sometimes they don't get any other cards or phone calls. During lockdown I regularly rang people from church to pray and sing with them. I liked cheering people up.

I absolutely love my family

Home and family

I am a real family person, I absolutely love my family and I am so thankful for them and for what they have taught me in life.

On May 26th 1997 my life changed for the better when my little sister Suzie was born. When I first saw Suzie I nearly poked her eye out, but over time my love for her grew; me and my sister are really close with each other. I loved playing with my little sister, but we did have some ups and downs like any sisters would. We call ourselves the crazy sisters and I love Suzie so much. She is the best sister ever and I am so thankful to God for her; she has taught me a lot.

Suzie studied German and Italian at Bristol, I missed her lots when she was in Austria and Italy. Then she did a Masters in Migration studies at Bristol University. She had fun in Bristol; she has a boyfriend Finlay and he is a lovely man and he is one of my best friends despite him supporting Manchester United. Suzie and Finlay now live in Coventry and Suzie works for a charity supporting people with disabilities. She helps people find jobs and she is amazing at it – she got me my job working with children with DS.

© Jay Crowter

On my wedding day with Suzie

My big brother Dan was born in 1992, and he is a fantastic brother. He has taught me that you don't need a megaphone when you already have a loud mouth! In our family videos he was very encouraging of me to carry on running in Olympic family games. I love Dan, he is an amazing brother and he is great fun to be around; he always has a way to cheer me up. Dan loves working with children with special needs and has a son called Josh who is eleven. He is full of joy and energy; sometimes I wish I had half his energy. He is teaching me to be a Liverpool manager on Fifa. He has taught me a lot in my life , he has taught me to stop talking as much—which never works.

My other brother is Tim and I love Tim and I always will. He is a fantastic brother. He has helped me block my internet from other people using it, and thanks to him I now like maths. To be honest, I used to hate maths, but when Tim started working for an educational maths company called Sparx, he knew that I struggled with maths so he set me up an account. Now I say to my Future Guides: 'Let's do some maths.' Yes, some of the questions are hard; for example, one of them was to work out 6/7ths of 56 and I was about to give up. Then my dad came to rescue! Tim is married to my favourite sister-in-Law Christie, and they live in Exeter. She is a wonderful lady who I am so proud to know; she is a very good cook.

Now the best till last. My parents are Liz and Steve and they are the best parents I could ever have. I absolutely love my parents so much. They have taught me a lot of things and have loved and cared so much for me despite my extra chromosome. I am so thankful to God for my mum and dad, they do so much for me.

Thank you mum for giving birth to me and for always being there for me. You have taught me so much, and have been the driving force in my independence and helped me be the best daughter I could be. I couldn't have asked for a better mum. You have taken me here, there and everywhere for my advocacy work and to all my medical appointments. And always put me first since I was born.

Now for my amazing Dad who has done so much for me. He has taught me a lot and has made me into a better daughter. He is the best Dad I could ever asked for. Whatever he does for me he never expects anything in return. I love watching Liverpool matches with my Dad, even though I do chat too much.

Chapter 13

Independent living

 I have always dreamed of having my own independence. Whilst I was at school I did travel training so I can travel on the bus on my own. I have always wanted to live on my own, I have seen my siblings leave home for university and I wanted to have the same freedom from my mum and dad as they have.

When I was eighteen, I got direct payments to employ a lovely lady called Bev to learn independent living skills, like cooking, cleaning, ironing, making the bed. When I was twenty, I moved into my own flat. At first, I was very nervous, but I settled in quickly and I loved it. Of course, I have had a few disasters, like flooding the bathroom floor, dancing whilst swinging my bag so much that the eggs all cracked and scrambled, and dancing and singing so loudly that I disturbed my neighbours! Whoops!!

I had a fantastic housewarming party; I had a lot of my friends to celebrate my joy and we had a great time. My brother Tim labelled everything in my flat and that wound me up because I knew what they were, so I went around taking the labels off one at a time and put them in the bin.

Although mum does the boring paperwork, I employ my own Future Guide. Her name is Brooke. I want to thank Brooke for all she has taught me and for teaching me the lesson of maturity and for making me the mature young lady I am today—Ha ha ha! I asked her fun questions in the interview, as it's important to me to have people who are fun to be around so we can have fun together. Me, James and Brooke have a lot in common. We do the jobs, then we have fun and let our hair down. We do the cooking, making the bed, cleaning the bathroom, hoovering, sweeping, washing clothes, taking the bins out. Sometimes we do the jobs on our own. I love going shopping with Brooke on a Monday. We are both shopaholics!

I loved being independent and having friends over for meals, having Bible studies, shopping, cinema and going out for meals. I was living on my own for four years before I got married and in that time I learnt not to grill pancakes, not to put dirty plates away, and that the internet can stop working! One time when I was in the other room Millie, my previous Future Guide, said 'Heidi, the internet is not working', I rushed into the living room,and it was working; Millie wanted to see my reaction. I nearly had a panic attack.

One time I was asked to be a bridesmaid for my brother's wedding, what would you do if your mum tellsyou to 'wear your heels in'? Would you wear them in or wear them out for taking out thebins? I wore them to take out the bins and completely wrecked them.

I have lots of friends who need extra support because of their disability, and some cannot speak or walk. But they are just as valuable and precious to their families as their other children. They have great lives too and are able to live independently as well. My friend Jane lives in a flat near me. She is severely disabled and needs support twenty-four hours a day. We have great fun having film nights and cinema trips. She might need lots of help, but she still has a lovely life and lives in her own flat and is very independent.

In December 2018 *The Guardian* Newspaper listed the top one hundred inspirational people with learning disabilities or autism—and I was among them.

A Week in the life of Heidi

Just to show you that I kept busy in my independent living, here is my blog-post for Monday May 1st 2017; however some of the things I was doing then are no longer running.

Hiya
I am Heidi Crowter and I am 21 and I just want to give you a snippet of what my normal week is like!

On Mondays, I have a Personal Assistant come to my flat called

Bev who helps me with cooking, cleaning and maintaining a clean flat! I feel I have learned by having Bev the absolute necessity of cleanliness. I have also learned how to get the cheaper things in my weekly shop. Every other Monday I go to a dance group or my youth group, Red Ds, which is the church youth group for people with disabilities— I love it

On Tuesdays, I go to work in Leamington which I love more than words, I work in a children's hair salon which I love, as I love kids; my role includes taking the payments, sweeping the floor, giving out stickers and lollies! Sometimes we get new-born babies in the salon which I read books to! I also do the social media for my salon. I volunteer at a Homework club which is at my church which runs from 3 to 4:30 and I love homework club; I love the kids and I am proud to announce that my role at homework club has been upgraded to birthday queen and listening to readers because apparently I am a good listener! (I disagree strongly).

On Wednesdays, I go to a toddler group called Tot's time which is led by a children's cafe in Coventry City Centre called *Coffee Tots*. It is a great Christian run charity which seeks to help parents with children, and afterwards I go to my church cafe and get a nice hot drink it varies every week! On Wednesday evenings I go to a drama company called *Ego* for my drama group and I love going.

On Thursdays, I go to my Zumba class which is South American/Colombian exercise class and I love going with my friend Gemma and then we have lunch together and then we go to the church which *Coffee Tots* runs.

On Fridays, I go back to Leamington and I do the social media at work and I do all the posts myself! I post the pictures from my boss's computer and I post them on with a little witty caption.

On Saturdays, I watch my Dad either win, lose or draw a football match. He plays in my church football team, and I am their only fan. When football is not on, I go to another Zumba class or go out with my friends!

On Sundays, I go to my church and I love going and worshiping my Saviour and Lord!

And so it continues! Thanks for reading,

Heidi

My first pay packet

Chapter 14

My faith and my church

I am a passionate follower of Jesus and God has helped me every day to achieve so much.

I was born into a Christian family, and I always attended church from a young age. I loved singing the hymns and I made a lot of friendships in my church, but my best friend in church is Paul Watts; he is my pastor. He was the third person to hold me when I was born, he dedicated me and baptised me. He has always encouraged me in my life, and I have really grown in my faith through Paul's sermons.

I started reading the Bible with my parents and I found out that God really loves me. As I was getting older, I wanted to know more about this God who healed me. I wanted to go to church more and learn more about Jesus, so I went along to some youth groups called 11up and connected and I loved it, mainly because I made a lot of friends, and I could see a little glimmer of Jesus in the leaders.

I also attended the youth group for people with and without disabilities, which is called Red Ds and I loved that as well. It helped me to learn more about Jesus.

When I was twelve I put my faith in the Lord Jesus and the verse that changed my life was John 3:16 'God so loved the world that he gave his one and only Son, that whoever believes in him shall not perish but have eternal life.' It was then that I opened my eyes to who I was before the Lord and that frightened me to the very core. So I knew I had to put my hope in Jesus, otherwise I would be heading to a lost eternity without God who healed me and died to save me.

When I was thirteen I was baptised and it was the best decision I ever made in my life.

I chose *The Power of the cross (O to see the dawn)* as my baptism hymn because I wanted people to know how much it cost Jesus to save me. I have been a Christian for fifteen years now but I still have a lot of questions and things that confuse me. For example, the mystery of the Trinity; but I know all my questions will be answered when I get to heaven.

I love singing the hymns and singing praise to my God. Because of my fantastic memory for birthdays, I write people birthday cards and make them feel happy and encouraged. I also do admin jobs for the church. I record the hymns so we don't have too many repeats, and I ask the leaders to change the hymn if it's a recent repeat. I tell them nicely.

My baptism in June 2008

I used to help at the church homework club, and my role was to listen to the children read their books and give them stars if they did good work.

I also love the lunch together we have sometimes on Sunday afternoons after the morning service; sometimes I bake a gluten free Banoffee Pie for dessert and I always get positive feedback, so I love baking it for thankful people. I still help in the creche every third Sunday. I help look after the kids and we have fun playing with the toys and singing children's songs.

At Christmas, James and me make the large card for everyone to sign to everyone—so we don't have to send individual cards.

My church is like my second family; ever since I was carried into the church I have felt loved and welcomed by people. I can really sense the love of God in my church and I don't know where I would have been without Hillfields Church, Coventry. They have really helped me in my walk with the Lord. When I first announced my engagement to James, they instantly responded with love and good wishes, and I felt overwhelmed at the love they have shown to me. When I was born, I nearly died often, but my church would always pray for me and they even looked after my siblings when mum and dad were at the hospital.

I have a lot of friends in my church family, but my best friend in church is my pastor Paul Watts. When I first met him we struck up a friendship, we are very close friends. He dedicated me, baptised me and he married me and James which was very special to me because he is very special to me.

My church is very welcoming to all sorts of people with and without disabilities and learning difficulties; the thing that I love about my church is that my church accepts everyone no matter who they are—regardless of race, gender or disability because we believe that the gospel is for everyone.

I think that churches all around the country should put things in place for people who have speech impediments and disabilities. My church has a lift for those who are in wheelchairs or have back problems, churches should be accessible for all no matter who they are.

I really feel at home at Hillfields Church. They have fantastic preachers, and I can see the joy in the faces as they preach because it's a joyful message. I also love James Young's sermons because he is very passionate about what he is speaking about and I can see his sheer joy in his face and he always challenges me and encourages me in my faith. I also love Paul Watt's sermons because it challenges my heart and it's based and grounded on solid truth.

To give you an example of how much I love going to church, here is my blog post for Friday October 6th 2017:

Hiya, my lovely friends,
Hope you have had a lovely jubbly day despite the cold weather! As you may know I go to a Baptist church as I am a passionate follower of Jesus my Lord and Saviour!

On Sunday October 8th we are commencing a new sermon series which I am very looking forward to how God will speak to me through it!

In the morning services we are studying Jonah, Jonah is one of my favourites because it always reminds me of this words in my fave psalm (139): 'Where can I flee from your presence? If I hide in hades you are there.' Jonah should have read this Psalm as he tried to flee from God!

I am mostly looking forward to the evening series which is on the parables of Jesus as on October 15th we are looking at my fave parable because I love the father's reaction when the son came back, he ran to him and showed him compassion. I always cry when I hear that parable because it reassures me of God's undeserved grace to me. I also quite like the parable of the sower because I find it interesting how people react to the gospel of Jesus.

My Favourite parts of the Bible

I love my Bible and I love every bit of it. But my favourite verse is John 3:16

'For God so loved the world that his gave his only Son that whoever believes in him will not die but have eternal life.'

If someone asked me: 'How would you describe the gospel?' I would go straight to this verse because it's the gospel in a nutshell and that was the verse that rescued me.

I also like when God said to Eve that he will promise a rescuer to come to bruise Satan[1]. I like that because it's like a glimmer of hope and a way out of sin, and it means that God doesn't leave us in our sin.

I have a lot of favourite verses. For example where it says that neither life nor death can be able to separate us from the love of God in Christ Jesus our Lord,[2] this gives me a smile on my face every time I read it or hear it preached on; it reminds me that there is nothing I can do that can separate me from God's love, and even if I disobey him it won't separate me from his love. It reminds me through the good and the bad God still works for our good.

I love where Jesus says, 'It is finished'[3] because it reminds me that Jesus has finished his plan of salvation, and has made a way for me to get to heaven; and the part where Jesus rose again, assuring us that he has gained the victory over death and that he has the keys to death and hell and only he can overcome hell. I also love when Jesus said 'On this rock I will build my church and the gates of hell will not prevail against it '[4] because it gives me great assurance that as we strive to build God's church nothing can withstand it.

I also love Ephesians 5:25: 'Husbands love your wives as Christ has loved the church' because it reminds me of Christ's love at the cross and how husbands should mirror that love to their wives.

Psalm 139:14 reads, 'I praise you because I am fearfully and wonderfully made.' This always cheers me up when I think about the current discriminatory law against people with Down's syndrome and other disabilities, that God has

---

1   Genesis 3:15
2   Romans 8:38–39
3   John 19:30
4   Matthew 16:18

made me in his image for his glory to radiate his character.

Psalm 23 gives me great comfort in hard times, and it reminds me that God has not left us on our own; it also puts my soul at ease because it reminds me that God leads me in a good way. Psalm 103 reminds me of all the blessings I have in Jesus Christ, and it really makes me rejoice in his kindness and for every blessing he showers on my life.

Sometimes I learn verses through real situations. Let me take you back to March 2019 when my fiancé James was admitted to hospital with pneumonia and a blood clot on the lung. When I first found out, I was so upset I couldn't talk and I felt distraught. Tears were trickling down my face because I was thinking of when I had pneumonia as a baby I nearly died, and I couldn't bear the thought of the love of my life dying. The verse which really helped me was Philippians 4:6–7 'Do not be anxious about anything, but in everything, by prayer and petition, with thanksgiving, present your requests to God.' So, every night I would cry to God to spare his life and that is why I am so thankful to God for the NHS because if it wasn't for the NHS and God, I would have lost the best thing in my life.

I also have a favourite book in the Old Testament which is Esther because she helps me in my campaigning. When I get nervous, on very rare occasions, I think of her courage in going to the king. I love her motto 'If I die, I die'; and I love the fact that she got everyone to pray for her, which is the same that I do—I get everyone to pray for me when I am doing my tireless work for justice in this land.

My favourite Easter verse is, 'I am the resurrection and the life he who believes in me will live even though he dies.' [5] I love this verse because it lifts my eyes to the day of no abortions, and justice for everyone no matter what colour or what culture and ability.

Joshua 1:9 reminds me 'I will be with you wherever you go', because it reminds me that I am not alone in my campaigning and my fight for justice for the unborn babies.

---

5   John 11:25

These are a few of my favourite hymns

Ten thousand reasons, really captures the essence of God's character and who he is, and it goes through the glorious aspects of his glorious character.

Fear not for I have redeemed you, was written by my fantastic dad looking back at the time when I was in and out of hospital with leukaemia. It moves me to tears because of my dad's faith. He had faith that God was walking with him in the fire of his daughter being really ill.

There is a hope that burns within my heart, reminds me of the hope that I have in Jesus; that hope stays with you through sorrows and joys. My hope in Jesus keeps me through the trials in my life and my hope in Jesus gives me strength to carry on in my campaigning when I feel like giving up.

O church arise and put your armour on, strengthens me to carry on fighting for justice when I feel like giving up. I sing this hymn and it reminds me of who I am doing this for and it helps me to have the hope of a better world.

The Servant King, reminds me of Jesus as the suffering servant and of the love he has for us and the willingness to serve us, for giving up heaven for sinful human beings. It boggles my mind that the Maker of heaven and earth would want someone like me.

Behold our God, lifts my eyes from the things of this earth to focus on the character and the awesomeness of my God and his sustaining power in creation.

Glory to Jesus, risen conquering Son, is joyful and jubilant and it reminds me of the wonder of the resurrection and the hope that one day I will be risen with him; it reminds me that my death has been defeated and I am free from the power of sin and that sin has no grip on me.

In Christ alone my hope is found, reaffirms my faith and it reminds me that my hope is found in Jesus so I don't need to fear anything and I can face anything knowing that I have an eternal faith in Jesus and it's a great hymn of confidence in Jesus and it reflects the story of the gospel .

When I survey the wondrous cross, has beautiful words and it makes me cry because Isaac Watts put it so beautifully. I love the last verse 'Love so amazing so divine demands my soul my life my all' because it's deep and challenging and makes me think about if I live that way.

I have loved you, what a mystery, reminds me of the wonder of God's love for me and it reminds me that God really cares for me as his precious child. It's also another one of my dad's classic hymns.

Hark the herald angels sing, I love the theology that Charles Wesley so perfectly put: 'Veiled in flesh the Godhead see'; it makes me want to praise God even more and it makes me full of awe and wonder that this baby is God in flesh which baffles me that God who doesn't need anyone would come for finite creatures like us.

O to see the dawn of the darkest day, this was my baptism hymn and it paints a picture of the Good Friday story and when I sing it I feel like I am there watching it happen and breaking down in tears at the love he showed on the cross .

There's a well of forgiveness. I love this, not because the writer is my dad but because I love the word 'well'; if you think about it, a well is overflowing and it's lovely to compare God's forgiveness to a well because it reminds me that God's forgiveness is constant and never runs out on me .

What a friend we have in Jesus, reminds me that I can trust him for anything and I find my true friend in Jesus.

My own hymn writing

When I first attended a Stuart Townend concert, I thought to myself: 'I want to be like him and write my own hymns'; so I now write hymns. I think the secret to writing a good hymn is to make sure the verses are based on the solid rock of God's word. I have written a lot of hymns and I put them in a folder.

In my hymn writing I try to put gospel truths in my hymns, and make them about Jesus; I also try to shape them around situations in my life and what I have learned through the situations. I also try to capture the essence of the beauty of our Lord Jesus Christ and all the aspects of his character. My longest aim is to sing my hymns in church and I want my hymns to edify people in love and to challenge them.

I love writing hymns because it's a good way to express praise to God and I try to reflect the words from parts of the Bible and the greatness of our God.

Here is one of my hymns:

Christ is the image
of the invisible God.
He is supreme
in everything!
Everything holds together
by the power of Jesus.

Christ is supreme
as God.
He held the highest
place in glory.
Jesus is greater
than anyone.

Christ is supreme
over creation.
All things were made

through Him and for Him.
He made everything
so wonderful.

Christ is supreme
over his church
because of the blood he shed.
Death cannot hold Jesus,
so death can't hold us,
so one day we too will rise.

Christ is supreme
in our hearts.
We want Him to have
the pre-eminence
in our hearts
and rule over our hearts.

I spend time each day with Jesus

On Friday June 16th I shared my daily plan in my blog post:

Hope you all have a lovely day as lovely as you all are!

As you may know I love Jesus, I am going to give you an insight to what I am doing in my quiet time. At the moment I am in Acts and recently I have been reading the sermon of Peter and the effects it had on the people listening. I am going through the Prospects series and at the moment I am learning about the first Christians in the Bible. I have also started buying some *Life Builder Bible study books*; the ones I am doing are Genesis, Romans, John and Philippians. I am loving my quiet time with Jesus. I also pray for those in the church family who are going through tough times and for those who are not yet saved!

Around the same time, I decided to take up some challenges to help me grow in the knowledge of my Saviour.

Challenge 1— Read the whole New Testament. So far, I have got to Mark Chapter 10.
Challenge 2— Listen to a sermon a day.
Challenge 3— Read the whole Bible
I am also learning verses from the Bible.

By the way. Talking of resolutions, at the beginning of 2015 I posted two new year resolutions on my blog: My first was to act my age! I was nineteen, but sometimes I don't act like a nineteen-year-old. This is an area for improvement and with God's help I will try and stick to this resolution. My second was to have a closer walk with God and to feed on his word more and to love and know God more.

On Sunday 4th September 2016 I heard an awesome sermon about true wealth and about what it means to be truly wealthy and rich. The preacher gave a very helpful illustration of 10,000 pounds pouring from the sky and that the world will go crazy for It. I wouldn't do anything. I would say, 'All I have is Christ.' I don't need a worthless passing thing that cannot satisfy. I know that 'godliness with contentment' is true wealth. [6] With the help of the Holy Spirit I will keep fleeing from the love of money until the day my Saviour comes again.

With dad in Croatia and quad biking in Croatia

Chapter 15

My marriage to James Carter!

My blog post for June 24th 2020:

'You may have heard that I am getting married on Saturday 4th July 2020 to a gorgeous man called James Carter who also has Down's syndrome, but that doesn't hold us back from spending the rest of our lives together. Due to Covid 19 we had to do some alterations for our wedding.

We are now only allowed up to thirty people in our church after the ceremony.

We are going to have a mini reception and our first dance as Mr and Mrs Carter and me and James are very excited to be married next weekend!'

© Jay Crowter

Every love story has a beginning

James Carter lived in Weymouth and attended the church where my second cousin, Matthew Sharpe, was the pastor. His wife told James about me, and my mum told me about James!

At first, I didn't know James that well; but I wanted to get to know him so I added him on Facebook and we started as friends so we can build trust and friendship. On 28th October 2017 we had our first date in Basingstoke. James made a very good impression on me, he greeted me with flowers and chocolates and he even checked the ingredients because I have Coeliac disease which means I am not allowed Gluten or wheat otherwise I will be very ill. He gave me my first kiss and I loved it— it was the best kiss ever. We went bowling and he beat me at all the games—he is very hard to beat. We then went to *Frankie and Benny's* and he paid for my meal. He is such a gentleman!

The moment I fell in love with him was when he decided to have a Bible study, because we are both strong Christians and we both love singing hymns. At our wedding the pastor said: 'Together we make a joyful noise and sometimes we are over enthusiastic'— I agree with him!

James went home from this first date and wrote his wedding speech!

After one year of dating, he asked my dad four times for my hand in marriage! Finally, my dad said 'Yes'. On 30th December 2018 James took me to my favourite restaurant, *Playwrights* in Coventry City Centre, and after we ordered our food he went down on one knee and said 'Will you marry me?'— in front of our parents, and I said 'Yes', while nearly crying because it was so sweet.

James is twenty-nine and also has DS, and neither of us feel that our lives are less valuable than other people's. A few months after our engagement, in March 2019, James was admitted to hospital with pneumonia and a blood clot on the lung. When I first found out I was so upset I couldn't speak because I didn't want to lose the best thing that has ever happened to me. It was then that my love for James grew stronger. Thankfully I got to visit him in hospital, and he was very weak. But then I remembered this Bible verse flashing through my mind: 'God's power is made perfect in weakness.' The thing that I love about James is that he is happy in hard times, when he saw me in his hospital bed he gave me a beaming smile—he has a gorgeous smile.

During this hard time, I learnt how to love James 'in sickness and in health'—good practice for our married life! And how to trust in God; the verse that really helped me was Romans 8:28, 'For I know that all things work together for the good of those who love God.' I knew it was a bad situation, but I learnt that God brings good out of bad situations. I also learned that the power of prayer changes situations, so I prayed every night for him while he was in hospital and when I phoned him the day after, he was getting better; that just proves the power of prayer.

The man of my dreams

I have always dreamed of having a man of my dreams. What I look for in a man is kindness and generosity; someone who is also a Christian like me, good looks, first-aid trained—as I can be quite clumsy sometimes! Someone who accepts me as I am despite my flaws, and who is a gentleman who takes me out for meals and who treats me like a queen; and a very good kisser and someone I can be myself around.

On Saturday July 4th 2020 my dreams came true when I finally got married to James Bryn Carter at Hillfields Church in Coventry. That was the first day that weddings were allowed after the first Covid 19 lockdown, and it was the best day of my life. We had planned a massive wedding with two hundred and fifty guests; instead, because of Covid 19, we could only have thirty. However, about ten thousand people watched it online and lots have watched it since! We are very thankful for the live stream. We planned a celebration the following May with all our family and friends coming. But Covid meant that didn't happen either. So, we celebrated our wedding reception with lots of family and friends at the Chesford Grange on Saturday 7 May 2022.

We were planning to have our honeymoon in Italy at Lake Garda but, due to Covid 19, on the wedding night we moved in together into our flat and had a staycation in Coventry. We had a lot of fun going to different places. The first day we went to Draycote Water and then we went to the cinema and had lovely meals out! We had a great staycation.

Me and James have been filmed by the BBC about the wedding and how we felt; we were also on ITV Central and so we are loving being a famous couple. Sally Phillips, the actress, presents Sunday Morning Live and we were filmed for that as well and it was so fun.

Our Future Guides helped me to learn how to travel from Coventry to Weymouth independently to meet James. My first journey was in January 2018, and here is my blog post about that day:

'Hiya, Hope you have had a great day! I hope you know that I recently achieved my goal of using the train on my own and I loved it! At first, I was trained with my Future Guides Millie and Bev and they really helped me to build my confidence in doing it and taking the lead.

I was a bit nervous as it was my first time but these words flashed through my mind about how God is 'The Great I AM' and that he cares for us, which really helped me !

Thank you to my mum for letting me do it!'

© Andrew King

Heidi and James at their wedding celebration on Saturday May 7th 2022

Honoured

On 11 May 2022 Alison Morley [7], one of our friends, posted her recollection of the reception. Part of her blog post read:

A funny thing happened the other day. I think I may have attended the best wedding reception ever. The actual wedding took place two years ago but plans for a large celebration were scuppered by Covid. Thankfully, the Bride and Groom could now be truly honoured by many more than were able to attend the original ceremony.

I've since been reflecting on why this celebration felt so special—like no other. For a start, the Bride and Groom had Down's syndrome. How many weddings have *you* been to where that was the case?

It was more than a celebration. More than a just a party. A joy filled day of people with Down's syndrome—and there were many—and people without Down's syndrome, all quite simply enjoying one another's company. All the usual things you might expect to find at a wedding: colourful outfits, smart suits, table favours, speeches—including the best one I've ever heard from a Groom, cheesy wedding songs and disco lights…. Simple extravagance.

Yet also quite profound.

Alongside those who were getting married, giving speeches or playing musical instruments, living their lives to the fullest, planning and dreaming of their own special day, was my daughter Hazel, who also has Down's syndrome. I am realistic enough to know that she is unlikely to realise those same dreams, even if she were able to dream them in the first place. She is far less able than many with Down's syndrome. Yet, in that wedding reception I felt a sense of love and care towards her that I've rarely come across anywhere else outside our own community. As Hazel wandered around the tables of seated guests in her own autistic, non-verbal yet noisy world, present yet elsewhere, I sensed a belonging. No one stared or looked away as they often do in these situations. They smiled. Not out of pity, but out of love. They reached out to her without hesitation. They honoured her just as they honoured the other

---

7   See also Alison's blog post on p.167

guests who had Down's syndrome. We did not strive for inclusion. That was a natural given. And though I joked about 'life goals' when she inadvertently led the Conga from her wheelchair, it wasn't a joke at all. Even the DJ said it was the best Conga he'd ever seen.

At breakfast the next day I saw other guests who also had Down's syndrome excitedly talking about when it would be their turn. Their wedding day. Even if they hadn't yet got a partner. They were now daring to dream the same dream.

This Wedding was not a celebration. It was an Honouring Ceremony. A safe place to be. An honouring place to be. Where the least became first. A day when people who have Down's syndrome were truly honoured, not routinely mocked, feared, shunned or despised. To honour is so much more than to celebrate. It is not dependent on any accomplishment, however noteworthy. The wedding was an honouring occasion. It was filled with love and kindness. I hope there will be many more weddings for people with Down's syndrome.

Yet, within the space of just forty-eight hours, this realisation came home to me and my family with a brutal bang.

My eldest child, just twelve years old and a young carer to her sibling Hazel, soon found that the Wedding Bubble had burst. Saturday's honouring of people with Down's syndrome, people whom she loves, turned into Monday's mocking of them. A fellow classmate, in their impatience over tech that wasn't functioning correctly, directed two words at my daughter—forcefully:

'That computer's got Down syndrome.' It was said twice, once to her, then to an adult. For laughs.

Except my daughter didn't laugh. She cried. She left the room in shock and missed the start of a test she had been about to take. The other child was taken aside, reprimanded and shown how their words could never be funny, only hurtful. How does a twelve-year-old learn to say such a thing? To target a group of people so thoughtlessly and for laughs? I can only think it is because they had heard it before. Likely many times.

Thankfully, restorative justice meant that heartfelt apologies were made and fully accepted. The child was genuinely contrite and felt bad. A lesson learned the hard way. There should always be room for a way back. Room for restoration.

James—my story

I was adopted by my lovely parents Chris and Bryn when I was nine months old; they absolutely love and adore me, and I them. They have told me all about adopting me. They had been thinking and praying for a long time about adopting another child, then one day my dad came home from work with some news, he had seen an advert in our local *Echo* from social services to say there was a baby with Down's syndrome (aged four months) that needed a home. My parents, brother and sister all sat down and talked and prayed about this baby boy. My sister looked up and said, 'I think we have done enough talking and praying, let's reply to the advert'. So, they did.

They met a lovely social worker, and she started to visit the family over the next few months. When the long process was over my family were very excited to go and visit me. I was being fostered by lovely foster carers. My mum and dad said they fell in love with me instantly and knew that they wanted me to be their son. My brother Ben and sister Esther spent so much time helping and loving me. I have a fantastic family.

I would like to tell you what Jesus has done for me. This is a verse from the Bible: 'For God so loved the world that he gave his only begotten Son, that whoever believes in him, should not perish but have everlasting life' (John 3:16).

Because I've been brought up in a Christian family I have always gone to church, I loved to sing the hymns and meet friends, but that was it! Then one Sunday I was listening to the Easter message about Jesus going to the cross and dying for me to take my sins away, this made me think about all the bad things I had done. I thought of God allowing His son to die on a cross for me, and Jesus rising from the dead, and making a home for me forever in heaven.

It made me realise I needed to ask Jesus to forgive me my sins and become part of his family, so I asked Jesus to come into my life and forgive me my sins. This changed me. I understand that Jesus is my Saviour and I have nothing to fear, for Jesus knows all things and I know my future is in his hands. One day I will be with Jesus in heaven because he is alive and when I die or Jesus returns, I will be with him, so I have no fears; I know I can call on Jesus and he will hear me. There are still times when I get things wrong and find things difficult, but now I know I can pray and read my Bible and I know Jesus will always listen and help me day by day.

One day I asked to be baptized which meant I had to go down under the water, this is a witness to others that my old ways are washed away, and I am alive with Jesus forever.

This is one of the verses in the Bible I find encouraging: 'Be strong and of good courage. Do not be afraid, nor be dismayed, for the Lord your God is with you wherever you go' (Joshua 1:9).

Some of James' family at the wedding in July 2020

© Jay Crowter

When I first met Heidi

It was an amazing day of meeting my best friend who I always dream of. We have the same things in common: we are both Christians and we go to church to worship our Saviour Jesus Christ, we love singing all the hymns and meeting our church friends that we love to chat to.

Heidi and I and our parents went to Basingstoke on 28th October 2017. We went bowling and went for a meal at *Frankie and Benny's,* my favourite bit was when I beat her at bowling. We all had a great time. I wrote my wedding speech when I got home.

I loved going on holiday to Sorrento with Heidi's family in April 2018. We had a great time. After dating Heidi for five weeks, I asked Steve for Heidi's hand in marriage. He said 'No'. I asked Steve three more times over the next year because I was eager to get my girl and my soul mate. Then finally in November 2018, Steve said 'Yes'. HALLELUJAH! Steve's face was really serious with his eyes of sincerity and Liz was in the background helping!

On 20th December 2018 I asked Heidi to marry me, we all went to Heidi's favourite restaurant, *Playwrights*, in Coventry. I went down on one knee and I said to Heidi: 'Will you marry me?' She didn't know this was coming and she said, 'Yes'. She loved the ring that I had chosen. Then we all had a nice dinner and dessert.

I woke up on my wedding day, feeling a mixture of excitement and nervousness and couldn't wait to stand at the altar. I felt a bit shaky waiting for Heidi to walk down the aisle, but once I saw her I was fine. The funniest bit was when Heidi put the ring on the wrong finger and hand. I have made a commitment to marrying Heidi because I thought to myself she was the one that I want in my life and I wanted her to be a part of my life and a part of my family. I also made a commitment to God in marriage, because I knew how amazing God was to have found me a gift of love in finding a beautiful, amazing young woman, Heidi.

This was my speech at the reception:

Hi everyone.

My wife and I would like to thank you all for coming today and making our wedding day so special. Special thanks to Paul Watts for agreeing to marry us.

Heidi and I are so delighted we have been able to get married on this day the 4th July 2020 our planned day! We didn't think it would happen because of Covid19 so thank you Boris!

I'm so happy to have married my lovely Heidi. She is my beautiful lady and I know we are going to be very happy together, I love her very much. She makes me very happy.

Most of all we thank God for this day. He has had us in his hands all through our lives, even before we were born. We trust God will guide us through our married life together. Thank you Jesus for bringing us together.

I thank my lovely parents Bryn and Chris for being so loving and kind and patient with me over the years and doing so much for me so I could be as independent as possible. I know that my mum and dad love me and will miss me lots, but I know they are very, very happy that I have Heidi as my wife. They also love their daughter-in-law very much. Thank you for everything, taxi service running me to my events and trains to visit my wonderful Heidi.

I had a wonderful time. I love you mum and dad very much and I will miss you so much. We will both visit you lots, so don't stop cooking mum—is it gluten free? Heidi always says that, doesn't she mum?

Also, I would like to thank my brother Ben and sister Esther for helping me so much as I was growing up and still do lots for me now, I know they love me as I love them.

This also includes Mike my lovely brother-in-law and Helen my sister-in-law and my nieces and nephew Erin, Evie and Noah; we have always done so much together as a family.

Thank you Tim and Lidja for helping me from the age of three when Lidja would be with me in Sunday school, as I sometimes needed some support!! She became an important part of our family. Also thank you to all my aunties, uncles, and cousins; and close family, and friends; for always being there for me.

My Church family are very important to me, so I would like to thank them for their love and support over the years especially Matthew and Karen, John and Grandma Chrissie who have helped me to follow Jesus.

Now my father-in-law and mother-in-law. What can I say? But thank you for allowing me to marry your gorgeous daughter. Thank you for making me so welcome and part of your family and understanding me. Thank you for all you have done for Heidi and me, and all that we know you will do for us in the future. We both love you, and of course Tim and Christie, Dan, Josh and Suzie.

I would love to thank and mention more friends and family, but I have to do this all again next year!!

So, a great big thank you to everyone that's played a part in my fantastic life so far. We both love you all.

It won't surprise you to know that I also gave a speech at the reception!

Hi everyone.

I am delighted to announce that I am officially Heidi Anne Carter and on behalf of me and James we would like to say a massive thank you for coming to celebrate in our joy.

We want especially to thank those who travelled a long way just to be with us today.

When I first met James on our first date in Basingstoke I thought that he was a dapper young man and very good looking—and he still is now.

He is also a fantastic kisser—let's change the subject before you run to the toilets and be sick.

I first fell in love with James when he took his Bible out because it's important to me for my future husband to be a Christian and to share my beliefs.

James is always thinking of others; he is always there to cry on when I need comforting, and he has a massive heart for everyone. James says many a time that he loves me just the way I am, and I love him just the way he is and I will never stop loving him.

I would also love to thank my little sister for all you have done for me. You are the best sister in the world; thank you for all you have taught me. I would love to thank my two brothers—thank you Dan and Tim for all you have done for me and for always being there for me. I would also love to thank my lovely nephew Josh for loving me as I am and being so fun and full of energy.

Thank you, Paul Watts, for marrying me and James and doing our marriage classes—we've learnt so much and we will apply it to our married life.

I would love to thank my parents who have done so much for me in my life. Thank you mum and dad for accepting me as I am and for treating me the same as my siblings and for always believing in me. Thank you for giving birth to me and thank you for all you have done for me in my life.

I would love to thank my mother and father-in-law for all they have done for me and James. Whenever I go to Weymouth, I feel like I'm coming to my second home. Thank you for treating me like a second daughter. I love you both very much and me and James will come and visit you —if you want us to.

Thank you all for coming and for listening.

Heidi

Married life

I would like to share with you how James makes me feel. He makes me so happy I can just cry happy tears! He brings joy to our flat and makes me feel like the happiest woman in the world. He makes me feel loved and special, and he is very good at comforting me when I am not well. We are enjoying married life a lot; we are happy and love living together. Even though we annoy each other sometimes, our love is still true as we have learnt that love endures anything. We are also campaigning together as a married couple; we are living the dream!

We do a lot of cooking. Our speciality is toad-in-the-hole which is a massive Yorkshire pudding with sausages and homemade mash and frozen vegetables. We also do some baking, but we do cheat and buy cake mixes because it's very hard to bake Gluten free as it just falls apart and turns into a mess, although they are still edible and delicious. Our Guide enables us to cook all these lovely meals and we have learnt some new recipes. We have learnt brussel-sprout mash and we have also learnt potato and onion skins, and they are gorgeous; we learnt them from my father-in-law who makes the best potato and onion skins ever!

Because we are clinically vulnerable, we had to do a lot of 'shielding' during Covid. But we have a lot of things to amuse us. We have been doing workouts, going on walks, singing hymns, sending birthday cards, having film nights, and because we love the same films we never have a disagreement about films. I do Duolingo which is a language website which improves my French skills; at the moment I am on a 148 day streak. We have lots of fun playing Monopoly. Then there's the housework! Which is tiring but it has to be done and dusted. We have our Future Guides coming in each day to help us cook the evening dinner and to maintain a clean flat.

We also have regular visits to Weymouth to see James' parents.

In 2020 I was nominated for Positive Role model for Disability at the 'National Diversity Awards.' Because of Covid the ceremony was delayed until September 2021. We went to Liverpool for this. I got through to the final eight from the seven hundred that applied so I felt so honoured to be there. I didn't win but I had an awesome night and I had a three course meal and it was beautiful.

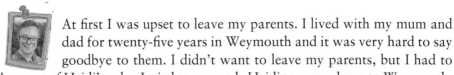 At first I was upset to leave my parents. I lived with my mum and dad for twenty-five years in Weymouth and it was very hard to say goodbye to them. I didn't want to leave my parents, but I had to because of Heidi's sake. I tried to persuade Heidi to move down to Weymouth, but she already lived independently and had a job near Coventry. She already had support set up to live in her flat. In some ways I really wanted to move away as my brother lives away too. My mum and I had a chat about moving away, and I said that my brother lives away and I want to be like him and live as independently as I possibly can. I then also said to my mum that I will be fine, and that Heidi will look after me. My mum then said are you very sure that you want to go away, and I said a massive YES!

I am enjoying married life with Heidi. We have lots of fun things together, we go out to places and look after each other; we watch TV together and watch DVDs. I really love independent living. We are both independent travellers;

This is me with my new mum and dad together with my brother Ben and sister Esther on the day of my adoption just before Christmas 1994

we travel on our own on the train, and the buses. We also have our Future Guide Brooke who helps us to do all the jobs in our flat and supports us both to do the cooking. But we can cook on our own at weekends and we are training to do a bit more cooking for ourselves. We also have joy and laughter together, and Brooke is amazing!

I have several jobs in Coventry to keep me busy. I work at a cafe every Friday morning at Longford Baptist Church as a waiter. I serve all the nice customers and chat to them. I also bring the food to them, take orders, and wipe down tables, and charm all the customers!

I also work at the British Heart Foundation every Thursday morning, sometimes I take the donations by the door, do some clearing away like hoovering, sorting out coat hangers, sorting out all the DVD's and CD's and sticking all the prices on them, and put them in boxes, and much more.

Heidi and I are Patrons of *Positive about Down Syndrome* (PADS) and we went on a PADS family day-out with Nicola, Tom, and Emily Enoch. Nicola runs PADS as Tom has DS and Emily helps Nicola run groups. We all enjoyed it so much. Heidi and I both were holding babies with DS; they were so cute. It was a very hot and sunny day, and we all had some nice food, YUM! And at the end of the day we sang 'Happy birthday to PADS' all together. It was a long day, but we both really enjoyed it. When we got home we both went straight to bed!

This was my 18th birthday celebration!

Hobbies and interests

If you're like me, you might have a lot of hobbies and things you like to do. I have a lot of hobbies.

I also love watching football. I am a fan of Liverpool football club. I have been supporting Liverpool all my life because my dad supports them because someone asked him when he was a child 'What team do you support? I support Liverpool', and my dad said 'I support them too' because he wanted to fit in. My favourite player is the Egyptian king Mo Salah because he is amazing, and he is by far the best player on the Liverpool 1st squad— better than Steven Gerrad and all the Liverpool legends in my opinion. My favourite Liverpool youth player is Curtis Jones because he scored us right through the next round of the FA cup, and he is only 19!

There are also other teams I like but don't support; for example I like Crystal Palace because they have a good solid team, and my favourite Crystal Palace player is Andros Townsend because he scored a banger against Man city.

Also, I like watching *Friends*, which is a TV show about six friends and all the things that happen to them on a day-to-day basis; it's very funny and it makes me laugh. I also love watching *Mr Bean* because it's about a clumsy man who does silly stuff and it makes me cry with laughter and it's just so funny.

I also love watching films. My favourite genre is romantic comedies, and my favourite actor is Adam Sandler because I think he is a comedy genius, and he also has a sweet side to him in his films and I think it comes out really well in his films. I have a lot of favourite films with him in.

I am a real Disney girl. I love Disney with a passion. It's the best chain films in the world because it reminds me of me as the princess and James Carter as the handsome prince and they live happily ever after. I love Disney films with songs in. I would say the best Disney classic is *Mary Poppins* because it's about a magical nanny played by the amazing Julie Andrews who is my favourite singer, along with Lidja Peel James's foster sister, because they both sing like an angel. *Mary Poppins* has some really good tunes which are bound to get you all bobbing. My favourites are *A spoonful of sugar* and *Supercalifragilisticexpialidocious* because you can sing along and dance along at the same time. and it really cheers me up when I am down. It brings a smile to my face every time I sing it.

James and me love singing, dancing, going to church, the cinema and going on lovely holidays. It's very nice for us because James's family live in Weymouth so we can have holidays there.

I also love musicals and my favourite musical is *The Greatest Showman* because it's about a very important lesson to accept people for who they are with all their failures; every time I watch it, it reminds me of James who accepts me as I am: as the bearded lady says in the film: 'This is me, take me as I am.' It always reminds me of my court-case and the fact that under the current law no one wants a baby like me. On the flipside, it reminds me that God accepts everyone no matter what condition they are.

Our life together

Chapter 16

Positive about Down's syndrome

 Heidi and I are ambassadors supporting the Down Syndrome Bill. We are fighting for better health care and for getting the law changed because I want other people with or without a learning disability to know and understand what the Down Syndrome Bill really is. We went to London and were very excited to meet Dr Liam Fox who is making the bill happen. The bill passed the second reading without anybody voting against it. We are helping the MP by finding out what people with DS want in the bill. We were very excited to go to a party in Parliament to celebrate it becoming the DS Act. The party was on March 21st which is World Down Syndrome Day.

Outside 10 Downing Street with Dr Liam Fox MP on World Down Syndrome Day 21 March 2022

The Awesomeness of the Down Syndrome Bill and why I support it

Hiya. My name is Heidi Carter, I am twenty-seven and I happen to have Down's syndrome but it doesn't define me, or hold me back from living a fulfilled life and I want that for everyone.

I would like to thank everyone on the All-Party Parliamentary Group for Down Syndrome for their help and all the MP's for agreeing with this awesome bill. I think it says something very powerful that MPs value people with Down's syndrome.

I believe that everyone should have great maternity care. When I was born my mum got great maternity care. They were very understanding about me having Down's syndrome.

I support the Down Syndrome Bill because I believe that anyone, no matter who they are, should have the right to good education and speech therapy.

When I was born, I had great healthcare that saved my life and I would like that to be the same for everyone else.

James and I are supported to live independently and get fantastic help.

We would love for other people with Down's syndrome to have an amazing life too.

I would love to thank Dr Liam Fox for being the brains behind this fantastic Bill. I look forward to working with him and others to turn this Bill into an Act.

Let's do this!

Heidi

By April 2022 the Down Syndrome Bill had passed through both Houses of Parliament and received the Royal Assent on 28 April 2022.

For one of the *Positive about Down Syndrome* campaigns, I filmed a short letter to encourage families who were anticipating that a child with Down's syndrome would soon join their family.

Dear future Mum

It's natural to be scared but don't worry about my extra chromosome, I can do a lot of things!

When I was born, my parents found it very difficult to come to terms with. My mum cried over what she thought I wouldn't do, she thought 'she'll never be a bridesmaid and she'll never get married' but man, they were wrong. Growing up I saw my brothers get married and wanted to be like them, and on Saturday 4th July 2020 my childhood dream came true. I got married to an amazing man called James Carter. I have no words to describe how much I love him and care for him.

My parents never knew I would get a job I loved in a children's hair salon, and have skills like doing the stock take, taking card payments, booking appointments, answering the phone, managing social media and much more.

Don't worry about your child who happens to have an extra chromosome being a 'burden' on their siblings— my siblings absolutely love me and have learnt a lot from me. They have learnt the art of patience because I may learn a little slower, and I have taught them how to live life, sing loud, have confidence and how to stay positive. My parents always saw my potential and treated me the same as my siblings. My brother and sister have even gone into teaching and charity work with people with disabilities. I am also an amazing aunty and role model to my cheeky eleven-year-old nephew.

They never knew that I could become an internet sensation and take the world by storm which proves that if you believe in us we will go far. Yes, I have an extra chromosome, but I never knew I would be shortlisted for a National Diversity Award, speak outside parliament, tell my story of independent living at the World Down's Syndrome Congress, have an influence on laws in different countries, be interviewed on loads of TV channels and be a voice for people with Down's syndrome.

Don't worry about the quality of life, I love my life! There are many support groups which can help people to gain skills and live independently, you just need people to help you unlock your potential and be empowered. Don't listen to negativity. My advice is to meet someone with Down's syndrome, see the person behind the chromosome, and love them as you would any other baby.

Hakuna Matata—it means 'No worries' in Swahili (from *The Lion King*)!

From Heidi

Down's syndrome and doctors

Late in 2021 I filmed myself giving a short talk to a small group of General Practitioners in Weymouth. This is what I said:

'When James and his mum talked to his GP about him getting married, the GP set up a few sessions with a learning disability nurse to help us understand more about relationships. They were really helpful. We did have lots of giggles with Charlie, the nurse!

Everyone should have a good experience with their GP because I believe that everyone should have good healthcare no matter who they are. I am very pleased that Weymouth GPs want to help people with extra needs and want to make the surgeries inclusive. Sadly, some people don't have a good experience because their GP doesn't talk to the patient, and they have a lack of understanding of that person's health. It is important always to talk to the patient because who knows the patient's health better than the patient?

On the whole, I have had great experiences with my GPs. They always listen to me and they talk to me, not to my parents or carers. I feel that is very important to have a good experience with GPs so they can get to know your health needs and help you understand what you need to do with your health.

By the way, all letters to people with learning disabilities should be in Easy Read. The first time I received a letter about my Annual Health Check I was confused as there was too much detail. Now I get an Easy Read letter and it is much better.'

But it is not all positive

There are so many false ideas about Down's syndrome and in a short video I and some friends responded briefly to some of them:

People with DS can't have relationships.

'They can, I am married and love my husband who also has DS.'

People with DS can't learn

'Sometimes we might need a little bit of a push (who doesn't?) but I passed my GCSEs and qualified in customer service and hairdressing.'

People with DS can't have jobs.

'Of course they can. I have had many jobs in retail, office work and media. I act and I dance.'

People with DS can't live independently.

'I did before I was married. And me and my husband still do. We lead an amazingly active life.'

Adults with DS are like children.

'That's patronising and insulting.'

DS is a serious handicap.

'It's not. We bring something to the world that other people can't. People come out with words like 'DS sufferer'. The only thing I suffer from is bad attitudes by others.'

DS is a disease.

'DS is a condition, not a disease; it is caused by one extra chromosome.'

Do you wish you didn't have DS?

'No. Why? It's part of me. Without it I don't think I'd be really me. I wish people would see DS in a positive light. My motto in life is: 'DS—so what?'

When you hear that ninety percent of women carrying a baby with DS abort it, what do you think?

'It's shocking and upsetting. Its discriminatory and makes me feel unwanted.'

Internet trolling

'Liz, I'm really sorry to have to tell you this, but there's a picture of Heidi being used as a Facebook meme. It's really horrible, mocking people with learning disabilities and making out they are like vegetables.'

I felt sick to my stomach when I had this phone call from a friend in April 2012. As I looked into it, I found there were other Facebook pages and websites abusing people with learning disabilities, using Heidi's picture, stolen from a

DS support group website, and those of other people. One heading declared: 'Don't listen to the guy above me, he's got Down's syndrome.' Some about Heidi and others were cruelly sexually explicit. *Why do people make and look at these kinds of things? What is so wrong with some people that they actually find this funny?*

Facebook later removed the pictures, but the pages remained. The pictures later appeared on other sites. When I drew it to the attention of West Midlands Police, I was told it was not a matter for their officers. We told the media about the issue, which involved other children too, and it was widely reported. Heidi and I were interviewed on BBC Midlands Today.

Heidi commented, 'I felt like I wanted to cry because these bullies don't have anything better to do.' Asked if it made her angry, she replied: 'A little bit, yes.'

I said, 'I was obviously really upset and very angry with the people and felt really sad that they couldn't do anything better with their time than to take the mickey out of people who can't always speak out for themselves.'

Professor Ellis Cashmore, who at the time was Professor of Culture, Media and Sport at Staffordshire University, was also interviewed: 'I imagine they are people who don't command any respect or authority from their friends in everyday life, and out of their frustration and their insignificance, they tried to distinguish themselves on social media sites. Sometimes they are cruel and sadistic and absolutely offensive'.

It was good to be able to make the public aware of how upsetting and insulting this sort of thing is. It's easy carelessly to mock people different from ourselves, without really thinking about it. Sadly, it provoked even more memes from the mindless and heartless authors of these vile things, but I'm sure it helped many reasonable people to better understand how this makes people like Heidi feel.

 Sadly, these views are reflective of the attitude of so many in society who ignorantly or wilfully scorn and humiliate all with learning disabilities. Richard Dawkins, emeritus professor at Oxford, tweeted his advice to a woman facing the ethical dilemma of giving birth to a child with Down's syndrome: 'Abort it and try again. It would be immoral to bring it into the world if you have the choice'. This raised a storm of protest, even from many of his own supporters.

In a subsequent interview with the *Independent*, Dawkins claimed that it would increase the amount of suffering in the world to allow a DS child to be born. When challenged how he knew this, he replied, 'I don't know for certain; it seems to me plausible and probably would increase happiness in the world more by having another child.'

The *Independent* wisely countered: 'What is actually immoral, though, is to look at a world not built for disabled people—including those with Down's—and agree that they are the problem, rather than the inherent inaccessibility and ableism [discrimination in favour of the non-disabled] that runs rampant in our society.'

Richard Dawkins later apologised for his comments, but the damage was done, and he still maintains that such people are a drain on the world, offer nothing and are not functioning members of society. Typically, Dawkins admits he has never met a person with DS! It is this ignorance of Down's syndrome and other disabilities that fuels negative attitudes and discrimination in society.

As Heidi herself insists: 'Go and meet someone who has Down's syndrome. Look at the ability not the disability—I don't like that word 'disability' because it says what we can't do instead of what we can.'

Voices that matter [8]

Sadly, prejudice is still being heard from the mouths of some medical professionals.

'Sorry, its bad news, baby does have DS; I've booked you in for a termination on Thursday at 10.'

'The midwife told us all the negative things about having a child with DS and she said, 'You're only twenty-eight, you're both so young, you should terminate and start again.'

---

8   All statistics in this section and quotes from people with Down's syndrome are taken from published research papers. Main source: *American Journal of Medical Genetics* (2011 and 2015).

'The only info I was given was a booklet, but it only spoke about terminating, nothing about having a baby with Down's which is what I expected and needed.'

Fortunately, other voices sing a very different tune.

'When the midwife rang again two weeks later, with the news the NIPT showed that Bailey had a 95% chance of being born with Down's syndrome, she again invited me in (with husband on the phone) if we had any new questions. Again, she listened, helped and advised. She was so warm and caring. We felt at ease.'

'The doctors were really reassuring giving us lots of booklets and assuring us our little girl will be absolutely fine'

'Everyone we encountered from doctors, nurses, health care assistants and cleaners, firstly always said "congratulations he is beautiful" that really meant a lot to us during such an overwhelming time.'

'We told the doctor we were continuing with our pregnancy. He then explained how many people with Down's syndrome went on to live a wonderful, healthy life and even got jobs. He then explained that some don't do so well, but explained that is the same with typical children as well.'

People with Down's syndrome also have advice for new parents:

'Take the baby home.' 'Keep the kid. Don't abort.' 'You have a nice baby. Please take care of the baby.' 'Don't be afraid. Your baby will have a wonderful life.' 'Love them, and they will love you lots.' 'The baby will bring you happiness.' 'Be patient because I found out that it is harder for me to learn.' 'Let the child have a dream and go for it.' 'The baby is just like you and me, just a little different.'

Surveys of people with DS show clearly how they feel about themselves:

99% are happy and fulfilled with their lives.

99% love their parents and siblings.

96% like who they are and how they look.

86% feel they can easily make friends.

85% feel that they help other people.

We wonder what those numbers would be for 'typical' people? I've never heard of a doctor or midwife regaling a new parent with a list of all the troubles and difficulties that they might go through with a 'typical' child. Surely any parent would be delighted if they know their newborn child would one day be able to say things like this:

'I am proud of who I am.' 'I work hard, and I'm happy.' 'I have Down's syndrome and I'm cool.' 'Don't label us. People with Down's syndrome do a lot of things.' 'If everyone was as happy as me, that would be great.' 'My life is perfect.' 'I really do love my life.' 'My life rocks.'

And what of the rest of the family? The gloom-mongers have plenty to say about this, but again the voices of personal experience are far more powerful:

'Think of the stress that this child will cause you.'

The stress experienced by a parent with a child with Down's syndrome is equal to that of typical families.

'Think of the strain on your marriage.'

In a study of divorce in families of children with Down's syndrome, other birth defects and no identified disability, divorce rates among families of children with Down's syndrome were lower than in the other two groups.

'Your baby will put a strain on your family.'

In 87% of families, everyone expressed feeling love for members with Down's syndrome.

'Will your existing children cope with a disabled sibling – you must think of them. Maybe terminate and try again?'

94% of siblings aged twelve and over expressed pride about their sibling with Down's syndrome and 88% of siblings aged twelve and over felt they were better people because of their sibling with Down's syndrome.

Tragically 90% of women in the UK terminate after a diagnosis of Down's syndrome. Surely in many cases it is because they have not been given a fair picture of the implications.

Like all people everywhere, those with Down's syndrome are not monochrome stereotypes, but dazzlingly different, a kaleidoscope of characteristics and abilities. In July 2020 a friend of mine, Alison Morley [9], posted on her blog 'Downright Joy'. The title of the blog entry was *Herons and Cranes*.

Herons and cranes

'I've been spending a few days in a relaxing and isolated place overlooking some fishing lakes. As I write I can see three, sometimes four, herons gliding gracefully overhead. Such extraordinary looking creatures in flight. And, once on the bank they adopt sentry status, scanning the lake for fish whilst giving a masterclass in superiority. Until they call out that is. A sound akin to fingernails on a blackboard. Beautifully harsh. Something about it grates and leaves the listener uncomfortable. It jars. Profound beauty and harshness held in tension. The herons take flight and with them my breath.

My daughter's life, her whole existence, is profoundly beautiful yet also harsh. We live, she lives, with the tension of these truths. And, as a consequence, she takes my breath away daily.

Many, even sometimes those in our own community, see the disabled life as something to be avoided. I know I did when Hazel was born. I've written about it before; how I hoped she would have some kind of 'Down's syndrome light' version of the condition. Not too bad, manageable, successful even. There are no limits on people with Down's syndrome is how the new mantra goes. They can learn to read and write, go to school, get a job, play sports, live independently, be models, actors, politicians, get married and so on. All true and all good, I don't deny it for a moment. They often do.

However, it is a profoundly beautiful life not because of any achievement or indeed any similarity to a life without an extra chromosome. Its beauty is in its existence. It should not need to be championed or given a reason to be accepted. It is already beautiful, profoundly so.

My early attempts to disguise Hazel's 'disabledness' thankfully and spectacularly failed. Hazel comes with an array of visual reminders of it: a feeding tube, the equipment, hoists, stairlift, adaptive chair, a hospital style bed, not forgetting bifocals for very poor sight and also soon to have hearing aids. Hazel is non-verbal and makes all kinds of noises that loudly announce her presence to the world wherever we are. There is no disguising Hazel! Oh, and she laughs—a lot!

Hazel has also been learning to walk. At almost nine years old she can now walk around the house or familiar places with gusto. Stomping and lurching as she explores familiar spaces now revealing previously hidden vistas and treasures. Her achievements are tremendous, and we celebrate them daily.

And yet. Remove her plastic clunky orthotic devices and her world shrinks once more, her weakened frail ankles collapse and she falls to her knees in a single step. Those unattractive plastic devices are, to me, of profound beauty and huge importance. They are enabling her to discover new and exciting things for herself, though her wheelchair is never far away.

Wheelchairs. Feared and avoided by many parents of children with Down's syndrome, particularly in the early years. I know this because I was one of them. So much so I opted for a buggy that looked somehow more—acceptable. I thought that having a wheelchair made her look more disabled. It does, but that is only a negative if you also hold the view that being disabled is something to be shunned. My assumptions were so very wrong. I mean, it's fine if you don't need one, but it's also fine if you do.

Is Hazel worse off because she uses a wheelchair? Is she worse off because she wears orthotics? Or is she discovering joy every single day in new places because she has them? Is she to be pitied because she is shortly to be wearing hearing aids or will people share her joy as the sounds we take for granted enter her world for the first time? And if they don't work, if she doesn't take to them for whatever reason, will that be seen as failure, or will she be allowed to live her life in the way she feels most comfortable?

To me, her disabilities just make me more determined to travel further into her world and see it though her eyes and ears. I desire to make her pathways less fraught with obstacles and trip hazards. Where those obstacles cannot be removed, I want to help her find another way over the terrain. This is what Hazel needs from our community, from those who care for her, from medical professionals, teachers, and especially Governments. Policies, medical research, social and educational opportunities that will enable her to live her best life; whatever support systems she needs, or we may need as parents, to help her.

What she does not need are assumptions that her life is not worth living. That she is failing or in need of pity because she looks more disabled than another. Nor do we need assumptions that, as her parents, we can do it all, that we don't need a helping hand from time to time. Caring is a very precious and undervalued thing indeed. Assumptions can be devastating, checking them and challenging them can bring change to entire communities.

A friend of mine often says: 'To diminish one of us is to diminish us all.'

Just this week I was reminded of the heart-rending story of a disabled community in Japan—the Sagimahara Institute—where, on 26 July 2016, a man attacked and killed nineteen residents and injured twenty six; thirteen of them severely. His intention was to 'obliterate' hundreds of people who he deemed unworthy of life and a drain on their carers. He believed he was doing society a service. The tragedy became Japan's worst mass killing since the Second World War. An extraordinary video called *Nineteen Paper Cranes*, tells the story so movingly and asks the question:

'Why does the world assume that a disabled life is not profoundly beautiful?'

I will not spoil the story—do watch, you'll be glad you did— but what followed in response to the killings was truly beautiful.

Landscapes can be harsh environments to live in and journey through, but at the same time profoundly beautiful. We need to adapt to their contours, their peaks and their valleys. Not circumvent them or leave them off the map. Or, worse still, destroy them altogether.

This is my daughter's disabled life, and it will always be profoundly beautiful.'

Campaigning

With Liam Fox MP for the second reading of the Down Syndrome Bill November 2021

Me with Lynn Murray from DSUO

Ali Fortescue from Sky News on Sep 23rd outside the High Court after hearing that we had lost

Máire Lea-Wilson, the mother of Aidan my fellow claimant, when we heard that we had lost our case

Chapter 17

Campaigning for equality

 In the UK, abortion became legal in 1967 with strict rules, but now you can abort a baby for disabilities, like Down's syndrome, up to birth. In 2020, two-hundred and twenty-nine babies were aborted after twenty-four weeks for serious handicaps.[9] According to the 1967 Abortion Act, this is the reason for abortion up to birth: 'That there is a substantial risk that if the child were born it would suffer from such physical or mental abnormalities as to be seriously handicapped.'

At the moment, when a pregnant mother has a baby diagnosed with Down's syndrome, she can legally abort it up to birth. When I heard that the law allows termination of pregnancy up to birth for disabled babies, I was really shocked and upset. I felt like someone had stuck a steak knife in my heart. I have one extra chromosome which means I have a learning disability. This is reason for abortion up to birth according to the 1967 abortion law. I think this is downright discrimination. It makes me feel that my life is not as valuable as anyone else's. As I have said before, I believe that all life is precious, we are all equal and we deserve to live, and that all life has value, and we are all significant in different ways.

I didn't want to stay silent. We found out about an organisation called *Don't Screen Us Out* which is led by Lynn Murray. The organisation is campaigning for the pregnant mums to get up-to-date information. At the moment their preconceptions are that children with Down's syndrome will never talk and they will never live on their own; but if you know me you know I never stop talking till I am asleep.

I have always liked speaking out and advocacy. I have been speaking out about Non-invasive prenatal testing (NIPT) since 2016. In fact, I was on TV back in 2012 and on Radio Plus Coventry on Thursday 20th March 2014 for

---

9   UK Government abortion statistics for England and Wales in 2020.

Down's syndrome Awareness Day on the 21st. Again, I did local radio after the *Don't Screen Us Out* in March 2016.

I was so sad when I found out that ninety percent of women abort if they find out their baby has Down's syndrome. Midwives and doctors often paint a bleak picture to parents antenatally, creating a culture of fear. It is very sad that when some parents are told their baby will have a disability, doctors put lots of pressure on them to terminate. The doctors often scare the parents with the details they give them. Sometimes the parents have to say 'No' many times before the doctors stop asking them.

I want people to see the person behind the chromosome. I think they should see the baby, not just a problem.

I wanted to do something about this and started with educating doctors and midwives in how to break the news to parents kindly with up-to-date information, both before and after birth. I spoke to groups of midwives and doctors at Coventry University on the Down's syndrome Association 'Tell it right' programme. I hope that by doing this they will stop scaring parents with outdated and often negative stereotypes of Down's syndrome.

Also, Doctors make mistakes. My mum's cousin was told her baby had a very small brain and would not survive. They refused any more testing and her baby is now a healthy twenty-year-old. A blood test or scan does not tell the whole picture; I might have Down's syndrome, but I can achieve and have a wonderful life.

My message to parents who find out they are expecting a baby with a disability is to carry on with the pregnancy. Because doctors are not always right and the baby is still a precious life.

The campaign trail
Westminster

In April 2016, *Don't Screen Us Out* (DSUO) organised a rally outside Parliament in Westminster. I spoke at the rally—it was really exciting and lovely to hear everyone supporting me and DSUO. I met Lord Shinkwin, who is a disabled peer. The rally was to ask the government to look into pre-natal screening. I wanted them to ask people with Down's syndrome how they feel about Pre-Natal Testing (NIPT) and to bring it in ethically. *Don't Screen Us Out* want the NHS to be ready for NIPT, rather than rushing it. They didn't listen. They haven't asked us how we feel.

I think people are trying to have the perfect baby but there is no such thing as a perfect baby.

The Nuffield Council of Bioethics published a report about NIPT. I went to the meeting when this report was made public—it was horrible. I was sitting really close to the people who did the report. I asked a question: 'How do you think it makes me feel?' But I was so upset that I started crying, so mum asked it for me. The answer was given to me by a disabled man: 'I understand it makes you sad, it makes me sad too, but the committee thinks NIPT is useful for parents.'

I just sobbed, luckily for me I was sitting next to the amazing Sally Phillips and she and my mum comforted me and I felt loved. Sally got her Bible out and showed me that verse 'fearfully and wonderfully made.' That helped me lots.

The report was 169 pages long with lots of recommended actions to help make improvements in screening. I was very sad that the government and the NHS didn't listen, and the actions were not completed before the rollout of NIPT in 2018. The UK government doesn't seem to care about the testing and how parents are so often steered towards an abortion.

I care, and it makes me feel very sad. I want everyone to know that we are just as valuable as anyone else.

Dublin

I spoke at pro-life events in Dublin in 2016 and on zoom events during Covid for pro-life charities, charities that support women who continue with their pregnancies. And at a conference for people with disabilities. James and I also spoke at a zoom conference about the Mental Health Capacity Act. We were telling all the people about our amazing lives and about how to speak to and care for people with learning disabilities.

In Dublin I said:

'I came here today to support you as I don't want Ireland to have easy abortion like we have in the UK. Everyone is equal in God's eyes. The Irish Constitution says everyone is equal in the eyes of the law. Everyone deserves the chance to live and have a fabulous life. It doesn't matter if you have a disability, your life is precious. I have lots of friends who have disabilities and they all have happy and fulfilled lives too. Keep fighting because every life is precious, has purpose and every life has meaning and value.'

Gibraltar

Just before Covid, in February 2020 we were invited to Gibraltar to speak. They had no abortion at all and were about to have a referendum whether they should allow abortion. I spoke to groups and the Chief Minister of their government to explain that a result of allowing abortion could mean that they then have abortion up to birth for disabilities. We had a great time and James did his first live TV interview— he was brilliant! The referendum was delayed by Covid but a year later it happened and abortion is now legal in Gibraltar. I hope that it does not become legal up to birth there too.

While we were in Gibraltar, we also went to see the Gibraltar apes. James was really scared of them because two of them came into the car and walked over him and made him jump out of his skin. On the other hand, I loved it and couldn't stop laughing because seeing the apes reminded me how great God is in making them just by speaking.

On the way to Gibraltar, we landed in Malaga in Spain and stayed in a place called Estepona. Our hotel was right by the sea, and we had a sea view from our bedroom window. Every morning when we woke up we opened the window and could see the glistening blue sea and the waves crashing on the shore and it made my heart smile that God who lives in my heart made that sea just by a voice.

We went out for meals every night, and one night we found an Italian restaurant, much to James's delight, and the food was beautiful. When I entered the restaurant, I felt I was on my honeymoon as it was candlelit on every table and on that night my mum decided to give me a quarter of a bottle of wine then I went tipsy and a bit loopy. Some advice: never give me a quarter of a bottle of wine. We had fun and some very late nights.

Northern Ireland

In 2019 and 2020 Westminster MPs decided to change the laws in Northern Ireland to make abortion legal, so that their laws were the same as the rest of the UK. I was asked to speak on the issue of abortion up to birth for disability. It was very exciting to be on zoom calls with Members of Parliament and Members of the Northern Ireland Assembly. One of the MPs, Carla Lockhart, met up with me in Green Park in London for ice cream. It's lovely to have famous friends!

On Tuesday 2nd June 2020 there was a debate in the Northern Ireland Assembly to allow abortion up to birth for non- fatal disabilities like Down's syndrome. I was mentioned thirty-seven times and I couldn't help but be proud of myself every time my name was mentioned. Thankfully, we won the debate, but sadly this was not enough to stop the law changing. It had to be voted on in Westminster so *Don't Screen Us Out* asked me to go to London to meet Peers and MPs from Northern Ireland and to present Boris Johnson with an open letter and a petition. The petition was signed by over 18000 people from Northern Ireland and asked the Prime Minister and MPs to let the people of Northern Ireland decide on its own abortion laws. Sadly, Westminster MPs voted against the wishes of the Northern Ireland Assembly and people and abortion up to birth for non-fatal disabilities is now allowed there.

Paul Givan, a Member of the Northern Ireland Assembly (NIA), decided to bring a private members bill in the NIA to 'remove Severe Foetal Impairment from the Northern Ireland Abortion Regulations'. I had lots of zooms with Paul and other Members of the NIA.[10] I really enjoyed finding out their birthdays before we started talking about the bill! This started in February 2021. I spoke to the Committee stage explaining why I thought this bill was important. Sadly, after lots of work by Pro-life MLAs, charities and Lynn Murray (DSUO) and Dr Liz Corcoran from the Down Syndrome Research Foundation, the Northern Ireland Assembly voted against the bill in December 2021. So now Northern Ireland has gone from no abortions, to allowing disabled babies to be aborted up to birth.

---

10   Christopher Stalford took over as sponsor of the Bill in June 2021, as Paul Givan became Northern Ireland's first Minister.

In my blog for Wednesday 17 March 2021 I expressed how I really feel in these debates:

'It makes me feel that I am fulfilling my lifelong dream to be accepted in society and that I want us to be accepted as I am and not to be seen as a ' Devastating diagnosis' or 'a crisis pregnancy'. I want to be seen as a human being, living life to the full and not a burden to society, I want everyone to see the Heidi behind the chromosome and love me for who I am. That is why I fell in love with James Carter because James loves me for who I am!

I have spoken in **Glasgow** and by Zoom in **Dubai** at the World Down Syndrome Congress about independent living. I spoke at the Dorford centre in **Dorchester** on World Down Syndrome Day in 2019 about independent living.

Five minutes' peace

The campaign trail involved a lot of travelling. However, with Heidi and James travel is never dull. Here is an example. After two busy days in London we arrived at Euston. I was exhausted. I hoped Heidi and James were too, in the expectation of a peaceful journey, but sadly there was no evidence of tiredness. I sank into my seat across the aisle from them, opened my sandwich and wine and told them 'Please don't talk to me unless it is an absolute emergency.'

I should have realized my peace would be short. Two minutes later James asked me who was going to book their train tickets to Weymouth—in a month's time!

I answered with 'wait and see' and tried again to relax. But not for long.

Heidi: 'Hello my name is Heidi, and this is my gorgeous, wonderful husband. What's your name?'

Jenny: 'Jenny'.

Heidi: 'When is your birthday?'

Jenny: 'June 28th.'

Heidi: 'YAY!! Same day as my husband, and Henry VIII.'

Jenny: 'Wow, you have got a good memory!'

(Jenny returns to her phone)

Heidi with great delight sees that there are three other strangers in our part of the carriage, so the interrogation continues.

Heidi: 'What's your name?'

Paul: 'Paul'.

Paul, expecting the question, answers: 'September 13th.'

Heidi: 'That's the same day as my dad and Roald Dahl. He wrote *Charlie and the Chocolate Factory*; I prefer the new version but James prefers the old. The new one is the Tim Burton one with Johnny Depp in.'

James realizes that it's time for his specialist subject: 'Johnny Depp is also in *Pirates of the Carribean*, *Finding Neverland* and *Alice in Wonderland*.'

At this point I am wishing the ground would swallow me up, but the other passengers seem delighted at the entertainment added to their journey.

Heidi turns back to Jenny, who comes off her phone: 'Jenny, where are you getting off?'

Jenny: 'Milton Keynes.'

Heidi: 'Wow my uncle and aunt live there. That's my dad's brother. Who do you live with?'

Jenny: 'My daughter.'

Heidi: 'What's her name and when is her birthday?'

Jenny: 'Esther and her birthday is April 20th'

Heidi: 'That's the same day as Hitler and my friend Lis. I tease Lis about having the same birthday as Hitler.'

James gets a word in: 'My sister is called Esther.'

Jenny goes back to her phone.

I decide, unwisely, to send a text to Heidi and James. This was a bad move because as soon as James receives the text he reads it out loud: 'Stop talking to the lady, she is reading a book on her phone.'

Much to the amusement of Jenny, Paul and the as yet uninterrogated other two travellers.

Jenny: 'It's fine. Don't worry, I am enjoying it.'

Heidi turns to the lady sitting next to me who seems delighted to have her turn.

You can guess what Heidi asked.

Christie: 'Christie and August 5th.'

Heidi: 'That's the same name as my sister-in-law. She is the best sister-in-law ever; she lives in Exeter with my brother Tim. Her birthday is November 19. August 5 is Louis Walsh's birthday and also my mum and dad's wedding anniversary. He deserves a medal for putting up with mum for thirty-two years.'

Hilarity all round!

The remaining passenger is ready with his answers...

Peter: 'Peter and January 1st.'

Heidi: 'Same day as Jack Wilshere.'

Puzzled look from all the passengers.

Peter: 'Who is he?'

Heidi: 'Don't you know? He used to play for Arsenal and Bournemouth. My sister-in-law supports Arsenal, all our family support Liverpool. My dad was a glory supporter and started supporting Liverpool as a boy even though he lived in Hastings.'

Everyone breathes a sigh of relief as the interrogation is over.

Heidi: 'Jenny do you want to play the connection game?'

Jenny: 'I don't know that game, but you can teach me.'

(Connection game is then explained: So I say poo, you say wee, I say toilet and so on.)

Jenny replies slightly nervously: 'OK.'

Jenny makes the mistake of saying rainbow after Heidi said sunshine.

So, Heidi replies 'Noah. James's nephew is called Noah. My dad wrote a song about Noah.'

A duet (I use the term loosely) is then provided by Heidi and James of 'God said to Noah, Never again, will I flood the earth with all that rain.'

Jenny: 'That's nice'.

Heidi: 'My dad has written lots of hymns.'

James: 'Yes, but he hasn't got any training unlike my favourite hymn writer Charles Wesley. Do you know his hymns, Jenny?'

Jenny confesses that she knows none. She is regaled with a list of Wesley's finest hymns.

She then asks 'Is he the top dog in hymn writers?

Heidi and James are momentarily silenced, so I reply 'Well, he was a few hundred years ago.'

Heidi: 'Ok where were we? Oh yes, its your turn, I said Noah….'

After a while Jenny asked us what we had been doing in London. Heidi explained that she had been at the High Court to challenge the downright discrimination of babies with disabilities. Heidi explained the different abortion time limits for disabled and non-disabled babies. Jenny was horrified and checked with me that this was accurate. We chatted about DS and the court case. So, another group of people who learnt about the discrimination.

Jenny is then allowed a few minutes peace until the train stopped at Milton Keynes and she could escape!

At last Heidi decides to follow James and put her headphones on and I have five minutes' peace. I remind myself never to go on the slow train again.

The Church of England Synod

 I had already spoken at the Church of England Synod in February 2018. That was the first time I met and had coffee with Sally Phillips. On that occasion I was so nervous because it was really new to me and I didn't think that I could speak to people high-up in the Church of England. I got up to speak and suddenly all my nerves floated away as I was thinking of Queen Esther and how God used her so mightily. I have always wanted to be like Esther and stand up for those who don't have a voice, and how she did one thing and saved a whole nation from annihilation; which proves that one voice can save thousands of lives who are worthy of respect and love no matter what condition they are!

I said then in my blog: 'Thank you to everyone who has been supporting me in my speeches and thank you to my mum who has been trying to calm me down for twenty-two years!'

On 4th February 2020 I spoke again at the **Church of England Synod** about the value of people with Down's syndrome. I did a sermon on Psalm 139:13–14 'For you created my inmost being; you knit me together in my mother's womb. I praise you because I am fearfully and wonderfully made; your works are wonderful; I know that full well.' I preached on three points:

The first point was 'You made me'.

God made us, God made our inmost being which I think is who we really are. So, we should use our whole person for God's glory. We were all made for a purpose to bear God's image. Yes, we may have Down's syndrome, but we are just as precious to God and valued by Him.

Every baby is beautiful, it doesn't matter what gender, race, ability or hair colour. He knit us together in our mother's womb. When you knit something, it takes time and love and it's delicate and intricate and God made us his most important creation.

We see that God loves us so much that he is interested in the little things in our lives: like the food we eat, the clothes we put on and many more. 'And even the very hairs of your head are all numbered' (Matthew 10:30).

God loves us that much that he sent his only Son for us: "For God so loved the world that he gave his one and only Son, that whoever believes in him should not perish but have eternal life' (John 3:16).

The Psalm also says that life starts in the womb and only God gives and takes away life. We should support and care for pregnant women and do all we can to help. We can pray for them, cook them a meal, encourage them that God loves them and their unborn baby.

God is the author of life and sustainer of life. 'The Lord gives….and the Lord takes away, blessed be the name of the Lord' (Job 1:21).

Therefore, we should respect all life from conception to death. We should not treat life as unimportant.

The next point was 'I am wonderful'.

Verse 14 says: 'I am fearfully and wonderfully made.'

We are all wonderful, not because of what we have done, but because God is wonderful. And he has made us wonderful. God still loves me even when I mess up. We all sin and disobey God every day.

Jesus died on the cross and rose again so we can be forgiven by God. When God looks at me, he sees the wonderfulness of Jesus, because my sin is forgiven through him.

If people say that you are not wonderful, or you are ugly, thick, disabled or stupid. Or if someone says you should have been aborted. Please remember that it's lies. Remember what God thinks of you.

Listen to God and what he says you are: 'I am fearfully and wonderfully made.'

Please will you now say to the person sitting next to you: 'You are fearfully and wonderfully made. You are precious to God'. *(WAIT for them to do it).*

Remembering that we are precious to God and our lives are a gift from God should make us happy and feel valued. Being fearfully and wonderfully made makes me feel loved and makes me think about what God says about me. That always brings a smile to my face.

It also makes me feel that, when other people don't have time for me, God always has time for me. He is always there caring for me, always there to hear my prayers and to forgive me.

My final point was 'I will praise you'.

In verse 14 it says, 'I will praise you because I am fearfully and wonderfully made'. Because God made us, our response should be to praise him with all our being.

In verse 13 it says, 'You created my inmost being.'

And Psalm 103:1 says, 'All my inmost being, praise his holy name.'

Because God has made us, praise should shape our everyday lives. Praising God is not only words or singing. If we want to praise God we are to show it in our actions too.

True praise comes from the heart. Praise means to show approval and admiration for what God has done for us. Obedience, praying, spending more time reading the Bible and telling others about Jesus, are all ways of praising God. Jesus has done a lot for us so we should return the favour and do all we can to show our gratitude in our lives.

Amen

By the way, while I was preaching, my pages of notes fell on the floor as I used them, so I gave them to the bishop who was sitting nearby. I didn't know that he was the bishop at first, for me he was just a normal person in my eyes who happens to have the skills to be a bishop.

Taking the United Kingdom Government to court!

I am so angry that the law allows abortion up to birth for 'serious handicap'. It made me feel not valued. So, I jumped at the chance when Lynn Murray, who runs *Don't Screen Us Out*, asked me if I would like to take the UK government to court over Ground E abortions. There is no definition of 'serious handicap', so babies can be aborted up to birth, who have DS, club foot and cleft palate.

We contacted a solicitor, who was keen to help us, and we started the process back in February 2020. Straightaway there were loads of phone calls from the media. I went on **BBC, ITV, Channel 4** and **Channel 5** and in lots of

newspapers. I have also spoken on the Victoria Derbyshire show about my court case.

It was all exhausting, but I love the excitement of it! We had to raise lots of money to pay the barristers and the court costs. But this came in from lots of generous people who felt that there should be equality in the womb. I was joined in my court case by Aidan, a two-year-old boy who has Down's syndrome—he is gorgeous—and his mother Máire Lea-Wilson. She had found out at thirty-four weeks that Aidan had Down's syndrome and was repeatedly offered a termination.

The court case got lots of attention on social media from the Down's syndrome community, people realised that it was not about pro-life but anti-discrimination. We found that most people in and out of the disabled community do not believe that this law exists. Then they checked it out and were upset and angry too and soon joined the campaign.

The law says twenty-four weeks for abortion, so it should be at least the same for ALL babies.

The court case was delayed by Covid 19 but we were finally given a court case date of 6 July 2021 and so we travelled to London to the High Court.

We had time to do some sightseeing and have some nice meals out and then we travelled to the Court. Outside the court I was being rushed from one reporter to another!

The reporters from **Sky News** and **Good Morning Britain** were both pro-choice and didn't agree with our case before they met me, James and Aidan. When they understood what the case was about and that it is discrimination, they both told us that they had changed their minds on the case. The Good Morning Britain reporter told mum that interviewing me and James was the funniest and most enjoyable interview she had done all year!

I didn't actually have to speak at the court which I was rather disappointed about—as I do like to talk!

The barristers shared my statement. I only went to the first half hour of the court case as it was really boring and mum thought I would find it upsetting. Sadly, someone at the court got Covid so we had to come home and the second day of court was held online.

After the court case we had a few weeks to recover, though there were still a few interviews for **Spanish, Italian** and **American newspapers and websites**.

I have met lots of important people while doing my campaigning: Victoria Derbyshire (a BBC presenter) even sent me a video message for my zoom hen party. Sally Phillips did a TV programme about the wedding, and we have spoken at events together. I also met the Speaker of the House of Commons, John Bercow, he was funny. I admire Lord Shinkwin, who is disabled himself; he has tried to change the law about abortion.

The verdict

On September 23rd we travelled to the High Court and heard that the *two* judges had ruled against us. They said that the law is not discrimination against babies with Down's syndrome or other disabilities and that it does not create negative stereotypes for people who have disabilities. I was so upset I broke down in two interviews and I thought I ruined them, but my mum reassured me that it's okay to cry when someone said that your life is not as valuable as someone else's. For a while, I felt that I was a failure, that all my fighting was for nothing and that no one loves me—which I knew wasn't true—and that I let everyone down.

Then I remembered that I had changed people's perceptions about the law and not many people knew about the law before; this thought cheered me up. I am proud of myself for coming this far and making it public. But I still managed to speak to the media afterwards. This is what I said:

> 'I am really upset not to win, but the fight is not over. The judges might not think it discriminates against me, the government might not think it discriminates against me, but I am telling you that I do feel discriminated against....and the verdict doesn't change how I and thousands in the Down's syndrome community feel.
>
> We face discrimination every day in schools, in the workplace and in society. And now thanks to this verdict the judges have upheld discrimination in the womb too. This is a very sad day, but I will keep fighting.

When Wilberforce wanted to change the law on slavery, he didn't give up, even when events didn't always go his way. And when the going got tough, he kept going and I'm going to do the same because I want to succeed in changing the law to stop babies like me being aborted up to birth, because it's downright discrimination.

As a strong Christian I thought about people in the Bible who didn't give up, like Abraham, Moses, David and Esther and I promise that I won't give up. I will keep trying.

It is a very hard and upsetting time for the Down Syndrome community, but we will not give up.'

Even though we lost we have changed hearts and minds about the law.

I have been nominated for a positive role model for the National Diversity Awards. I also influence different countries' laws. In 2019 Northern Ireland refused abortion up to birth; however, Northern Ireland is not an independent country, so their laws have to get approved by Westminster.

On the day of the court judgement, I met the lovely Ruth Madeley who is an actress, she has spina bifida and is in a wheelchair. She was very upset when she heard the court case judgement. We have also shown everyone that Down's syndrome is not something to be scared of and that people with Down's syndrome live happy, amazing, fulfilled and independent lives!

We found when talking to the media and friends and family that most people were on our side. Often the people who commented negatively on the court case had not understood it. They hadn't read or listened to the articles properly. There were lots of very negative and horrible comments from the British Pregnancy Advisory Service and Antenatal Results and Choices.

But mum and other people in the campaign answered them, so I just ignored them.

We asked the judges if we could appeal their judgement but they said no. So, next we asked the Court of Appeal if they will hear our appeal, and on 8 March 2022 we had a two-hour oral hearing to persuade them to let us appeal. This is my blog about it:

Hiya my lovely Friends

As you may know I have been taking the UK government to court as at the moment the law states that a baby with Down's syndrome and other non-fatal disabilities (for example, cleft palette, club foot which are easily corrected) is up to birth, but a baby without a disability is twenty-four weeks. This is downright discrimination. Last Tuesday we went to the Court of Appeal and we have won the right to appeal on the grounds of discrimination.

I was able to speak in the court, much to my surprise. I was very honoured as it's unusual to be allowed to speak in this type of court. This is what I said:

'I am twenty-six and I happen to have Down's syndrome, but that doesn't hold me back from living a fun and fulfilled life. The law that allows abortion up to birth makes me feel that I am not wanted and not loved. It makes me feel not valued, and that people don't want babies like me.

I think that the law is downright discrimination. People like me should not be discriminated against.

When the Abortion Act was made there was no Disability Act. People did not understand disability very well. Now because of the Disability Act we should be treated equally after birth. Please hear our appeal so all babies can be treated equally and all the time—however many chromosomes they have.

So please let us appeal and change the law to make us all equal. I want people to see us as people, and equals, and not just a burden.'

Thanks for reading

Heidi.

Heidi cuddling baby Elouise Poulton who also has Down's syndrome

On the 13th July 2022 our court case was heard in the Court of Appeal; it went well and I felt the head judge was very good and that he was interested in my case. We will find out the result around October.

Millions of people have heard me and Máire speak about the court case. Some of those will be women who find out one day that they are carrying a baby with Down's syndrome. I firmly believe that at least some of those women will come to a different decision because of what they have heard and will continue with the pregnancy. Whatever the final result of the court, that is a massive victory.

We are not going to give up. I think that all human life is valuable and should be treated with respect, however many chromosomes we have!

Outside the Court of Appeal with our Solicitor after winning the right to appeal the decision of the High Court

Resources relating to Down's syndrome

Don't Screen Us Out
https://dontscreenusout.org

Working to build a United Kingdom where people with DS are equally valued and have an equal chance of being born.

Down's Syndrome Research Foundation UK
https://www.dsrf-uk.org

Our vision is a long, healthy, happy life for people with DS and a passion for the very best evidence-based interventions

Down Syndrome Education International
https://www.down-syndrome.org/en-gb

Working to improve early intervention & education for children with DS.

Looking Up Books
https://www.cdssg.org.uk/looking-up-book

A series of books to help children with DS and their families.

Positive about Down Syndrome
https://positiveaboutdownsyndrome.co.uk

Online support from other parents, training for medical professionals.

Mencap
https://www.mencap.org.uk
A charity for people with a learning disability and their families and carers.

Wouldn't change a thing
https://www.wouldntchangeathing.org

"Creating a world where negative perceptions of DS are a thing of the past through media campaigns and support to parents."

Future of Down's
https://www.facebook.com/groups/futureofdowns

A Facebook support group

Teach Me Too
https://www.teachmetoo.org.uk/teach-me-too

Online library of videos and resources all designed around the specific learning profile of children with DS.

The Lejeune Clinic
https://www.lejeuneclinic.com

Early intervention sessions for babies and children with DS.

Down's Syndrome Association
https://www.downs-syndrome.org.uk

Down's Syndrome Scotland
https://www.dsscotland.org.uk